How to Stop Procrastinating

Developing Discipline With Hacks,

Case Studies, Apps And Tools That

Can Help Fight Procrastination

And Get More Done In Less Time

Includes Step By Step 66 Day Plan
to Stop Procrastination Today

DAN LOPEZ

Table of Contents

How to Stop Procrastinating

What Is Procrastination?

Procrastination, simply put, is the habit of putting off until later what you could, or should, be doing now. Procrastination can be seen in all areas of life—in the workplace, in studies, or at home.

Studies estimate that approximately 20% of us are chronic procrastinators. That means 1 in 5 people struggle with motivation and self-discipline when it comes to getting things done, and are therefore faced with the often debilitating and severe consequences of this self-destructive habit.

People who procrastinate are often labeled by others as lazy or incompetent. In many instances, these negative impressions also describe how procrastinators feel about themselves.

The Consequences of Procrastination

The consequences of procrastination can be varied and often severe.

The analogy of a credit card can be used. Where time is a currency, a procrastinator borrows time again and again, but eventually, the bill comes, and there is no time left.

There is always fall-out from procrastination, whether the outcome is personal, academic, professional, physical, or emotional consequences.

Consequences can include:

- Increased stress and pressure
- Insomnia
- Poor self-esteem
- Decline in work quality
- Wasted time that could be spent productively
- Missed opportunities
- Failing to reach true potential in the study, the workplace, or personal life
- Negative impact on work and personal relationships.

While procrastination may be a very common habit, it is generally agreed that procrastination is self-defeating behavior. Putting off important tasks due to 'not feeling like it', feeling anxiety over the enormity of the task, or being distracted by other things only causes the above-mentioned consequences to mount, and eventually become overwhelming and destructive.

The Three Types of Procrastinator

According to *Psychology Today* (Procrastination, n.d.), there are three types of procrastinators.

1) The Thrill-Seeker
2) The Avoider
3) The Indecisive Procrastinator.

Read the following definitions and see which type you

identify with the most. You may find that you recognize in yourself characteristics from more than one or all three types.

The Thrill-Seeker

Marcus

"Marcus looks at the clock. He has a college assignment worth 10% of his overall grade due in tomorrow and it's already 9pm. He looks at his paused video game and wonders whether he should get started on the assignment.

After a moment, he shrugs and continues his game. Marcus has been a lifelong procrastinator and has never missed a deadline. He knows that he could start at ten, eleven, or midnight and still get it done.

Why miss out on a couple of hours of gaming? He'll be more relaxed if he unwinds for a while now, anyway. He'll get it done. He always does."

Marcus has the ability to complete the task at hand. He has nothing more pressing to do. He's got plenty of time to create something great. However, he has confidence he'll get it done. He's not too bothered at the idea that it might end up being a rush-job.

Thrill-seeking procrastinators enjoy the thrill of completing a task at the last minute. They enjoy using their supposed 'free time' to do other things and then jump to the task just before it's too late.

<u>The Avoider</u>

Laura

"Laura's boss has given her until the end of the week to do market research and create market projections for a proposed new product line. It's her first time heading a marketing project and she's been putting off getting started. Truth be told, she doesn't know where to begin. She'll have to do some research on how to do research before she can even get started...And projections? Her math skills are a bit shaky. What if she messes it up?

A group email pops up on her screen. The team has asked if someone can go grab more milk for the staff fridge. Laura volunteers. A cup of coffee might just do the trick..."

Laura's terrified of doing a bad job of her project, so she's putting off doing it at all costs. She's got to do so much groundwork before she can even begin. Every time she thinks about how much there is to do and how many ways it can go wrong, she starts to panic.

Avoiders procrastinate because they're intimidated by

the task and the results of completing said task. They may think they lack the skill to do what is required or are fearful of doing a job poorly.

The Indecisive Procrastinator

Phil

"Phil has written dozens of notes and organized, re-organized and color-coded them. They didn't look great so he tried them in a different font. He was struggling to concentrate so he mounted them on study cards.

He's done some good research and has an idea of the paper he wants to write, but it's worth a lot of credit, so it needs to be just right. He tries putting the study cards into order to find the right structure for the essay.

Do you know what would really make the paper pop? A few great quotes. Phil fires up the computer and starts to search for some great citations to pad out the unwritten essay."

Phil is a meticulous and ambitious student. He's desperate to make his essay perfect but he can't settle on the right way to do that, so he focuses on the far less important minutiae without getting started on the main task and refining the details when he's finished.

Indecisive procrastinators fail to get things done because they're unable to make a decision. This can be because they don't want to take responsibility for the outcome of their task, or because they have a perfectionist streak that makes it hard to risk any decision at all in case it is not perfect.

Am I a Procrastinator?

If you have chosen to read this book, it is likely that you are already aware that you have problems with focus, self-motivation or seeing a task through to the end. You may be disappointed because you've missed opportunities, are failing to complete tasks to the best of your abilities, or are otherwise starting to feel the negative effects of procrastination in your life.

This book has been designed for the self-aware procrastinator. The following chapters will lay out the reasons why people procrastinate, how to recognize the pattern of procrastination, and outline some practical steps that can be taken to break the cycle of putting off tasks until later, tomorrow, or never.

You will learn that you don't need motivation—only discipline. You will also discover that there are things you can do to take back control over your schedule and reach

your full potential by using your time productively and efficiently.

How to Recognize the Warning Signs of Procrastination

The Procrastinator Stereotype

People often imagine procrastinators as people who are late, do poor work, and are messy, lazy, and disorganized.

However, although some procrastinators may show some of these traits, many procrastinators hide in plain sight and suffer from internal feelings of pressure, stress, and discontentment while seeming to be keeping up to those around them.

Procrastinators can have excellent time management skills, be exceptionally bright and hard-working, arrive on time, and meet deadlines.

However, a chronic procrastinator will recognize the trait in themselves as they may be suffering from the consequences of procrastination, such as increased stress and pressure, poor self-esteem, wasted time that could be spent productively and failing to reach the full potential they know they have within them.

So, how can you tell if you are a procrastinator?

The warning signs of procrastination

Below is a long list of common traits and emotions that chronic procrastinators will recognize. How many apply to you?

- Easily distracted
- Lack of motivation
- Low self-esteem
- Repeated failure to achieve goals
- Decline in work performance
- Problems in personal life due to unaddressed issues
- Feelings of being overwhelmed, stressed, or under pressure
- Self-identifying, or being labeled by others, as lazy or incompetent
- You blame a lack of motivation or self-discipline for many of your problems
- All your deadlines constantly seem to come at once
- Workloads that others seem to carry easily seem really difficult for you to maintain
- Even though you seem to have time in your schedule, you never get things done
- There are half a dozen things on your to-do list at any one time
- You always leave tasks until the very last minute

- You have a lot of things on your bucket list that you never begin
- Your personal space or workspace is disorganized
- Conversely, your personal space or workspace is incredibly tidy—you often occupy yourself with smaller, easier tasks, such as cleaning, rather than embarking on bigger, more important projects
- You fantasize about achievable goals, such as losing weight or saving money, but never take active steps to achieve these goals, or give up early on attempts to achieve them
- You believe you work best when a deadline is right on top of you
- You are discontent in areas of your work and personal life
- You are in the habit of wishing rather than doing
- You often find yourself thinking things are easier said than done
- You often find yourself feeling jealous of people who seem to have it all; those who seem to be

able to balance everything they need to do effortlessly

- You can't complete tasks if you're not 'in the zone'

- Tasks often take longer than you anticipate, leaving you feeling under pressure

- You get mad at yourself for not getting on with tasks you know need to be done

- You avoid committing to deadlines wherever possible

- You have extremely high standards

- You care intensely about others' opinions of your work

- The tasks you need to complete seem overwhelming or impossible to achieve

- You often bury your head in the sand when there are important things to be done

- You find it much easier to prepare for a task than to actually complete the task itself

- You have the desire to complete a task and recognize its importance, but can't muster the willpower to get it done

- You think to yourself how great things would be if you could just *knuckle down*

- You often regret delaying tasks and experience consequences for putting them off.

As you can see, there are dozens of warning signs that you might be a procrastinator. If you identify with several of the points above or identify with one of the points strongly, then you are probably one of the 20% of adults who identify procrastination as a key issue in their lives.

So, you've recognized you have a problem with procrastination. What now?

This book outlines the reasons why people procrastinate, going beyond common sense and really digging into the psychology of procrastination.

Once you understand the reasons behind your habit of putting things off, you can start to find the right tools and resources to break the pattern.

This book is just one of those resources.

Read on to better identify your specific patterns of procrastinating behavior and correspond them to the best solutions for defeating those patterns.

The most important thing to remember is that procrastination is not an indomitable beast. It is possible to develop the skills and discipline to overcome it and build a less stressful and more productive lifestyle.

Reasons Why People Procrastinate

Introduction

The general population has a very superficial understanding of the psychology of procrastination. The fact is, the reasons people procrastinate are rooted in deeper psychological causes than people understand. We will explore some of these in this chapter.

Partial Naivete

> *Chloe happily works on her company's social media pages. It's her favorite part of the job. She loves creating posts and replying to all the comments. It's easy and fun.*
>
> *She glances at the clock. It's 3pm and she must have that accounts report completed by 5pm.*
>
> *She's great at reports. They only take twenty minutes, tops. She'll come back to it in an hour or so and have plenty of time to get it done.*

One explanation for why people procrastinate is the idea of partial naivete (Rabin, 2001).

This term describes the habit of a procrastinator to being aware that if they delay a task, they will have self-control problems in completing the task in the future.

However, the procrastinator underestimates how much they will struggle when that later time comes.

These procrastinators fall into two types: sophisticated and naïve.

The sophisticated procrastinator is fully-aware that they will experience self-control problems at this later time, while the naïve procrastinator completely underestimates or fails to take into account this possibility.

A naïve procrastinator is overly optimistic when it comes to judging how long a task will take in the future, and therefore will happily delay said task, believing they'll have the time to complete it before the deadline. This belief that they are on schedule and have the time to complete the task well is a key attributor to the habit of procrastination.

Chloe is a naïve procrastinator. She hasn't taken into consideration that today's accounts report may be more complicated than usual, or that there may be an issue or error she has to overcome. Her optimism and confidence in the ease of the task and her own abilities have led her to procrastinate and delay getting the report done.

Consider: Do you ever put tasks off because you think they'll be easy or quick? Do you often underestimate how long tasks take and end up under pressure or late in completing tasks?

Fear of failure

Miguel is a struggling college student who is just getting by with his grades. He has an essay to complete and he just can't get started. If his past grades are anything to go by, this essay is doomed to fail.

Every time he thinks about starting, he feels sick. This feeling of dread takes over and even though he knows how important the assignment is, he finds himself burying his head in the sand.

A study at the University of Vermont conducted a study on procrastination among college students and completed a factor analysis of the reasons why these students procrastinated (Laura J. Solomon, 1984).

The study found that almost 50% of students' procrastination was due to fear of failure. These students worried about meeting others' expectations, not getting something 'just right', or lacking confidence in their own ability.

Consider: How often do you put off a task because you're worried your work just won't be good enough?

Aversion

> *Evelyn should be writing her report by now. But you know what? She just can't be bothered. It's a long and boring task and she can't bring herself to get out of bed and get on with it.*

Only 18% of students in the Vermont study procrastinated due to aversion of laziness. This is a surprisingly low figure considering how many people would consider laziness to be the root of procrastination.

In fact, only 1 in 5 procrastinators put off work due to laziness or simply not wanting to do the task. However, this figure is still a significant factor in procrastination.

Consider: How often do you put something off for no other reason than you don't want to do it?

Dependency

> *Laura hangs around by her colleague's desk hopefully.*

> *"Have you done your bit on the Excel report yet?" She asks.*

> *Robin rolls his eyes. He's used to Laura's hinting. "I can't help you right now, Laura. I'm up to my eyeballs in*

my own work."

"Could you just show me how to insert that formula again?"

"Fine. Sit down and I'll show you."

Some procrastinators don't have the capacity to work under their own steam. They depend heavily on others to hold their hand through tasks, to guide them and help them.

They may delay projects while waiting for help or because they've convinced themselves they can't do something alone.

Consider: Do you ever lean too heavily on others to support you in your tasks? Do you rely on a parent, spouse, colleague or friend to help you with personal tasks or work projects?

Avoiding the state of anxiety

Hilary has to finish filling out her divorce forms but hasn't got around to it. She knows that when she begins, it's all going to come rushing back—the feelings of worthlessness, the memories of her husband cheating, the panic about how to divide up their possessions...As long as she doesn't think about the

> *divorce, she can function. She just*
> *can't handle it right now.*

All kinds of tasks can incite anxiety; filling out tax returns, confronting an issue, sorting through a deceased relative's estate, starting a diet... Different people will feel anxiety around different subjects, but the fact stands that nobody likes to feel anxious.

In situations where a person knows a certain task will induce anxiety, they may put off a task as a form of self-protection, avoiding the feeling of panic and anxiety they know is coming.

Consider: Does the thought of completing a certain task fill you with dread? Are you putting off doing something because you know it will be distressing, upsetting, or emotionally challenging?

The Hot-Cold Empathy Gap

> *Liam just found out the money his*
> *best friend borrowed to 'pay for his*
> *dog's medicine' was actually used to*
> *buy a new games console. He's*
> *furious.*
>
> *Despite how angry Liam is, he's got*
> *an exam to study for. He puts it off.*
> *There's no way he could study when*
> *he's feeling this mad.*

The Hot-Cold Empathy Gap is a psychological term used to describe the way that we can't predict how our mood or temperament may change and affect our capacity for future tasks (Hollingworth, 2015).

When we are in a 'hot state' (angry, restless, hungry, distressed, etc.), we may find that we are incapable of committing to important tasks. However, when we are in a 'cold state' (calm, content, happy, etc.), we may find it really easy to get things done.

The problem is, we can never predict ahead of time whether we will be in a hot or cold state at any given time.

In the example above, Liam has scheduled a time for exam preparation, but now he's putting off doing it because he's too angry to do it. He expected to be in a cold state but has found himself in a hot state when the times to get to work come along.

This Empathy Gap can be a major cause of procrastination. Even though we planned our time well and thought ahead, there was no way to account for how our mood would be when the time came. As Liam found, this empathy gap can destroy the best-laid plans.

Consider: Does your mood often affect whether you undertake a task? Do you often break away from a set schedule because you're too angry, upset, or demotivated when the time comes for the task to be undertaken?

Rebellion against authority

> *Lucy doesn't know why she procrastinates; all she knows is that she feels satisfied when she does. It feels good to control your own schedule, doesn't it? She's a grown woman. If she wants to sit and watch Netflix instead of writing that dissertation, that's her call.*

Research has shown that there is a correlation between those who were raised with authoritarian parents and procrastination in adulthood (Timothy A. Pychyl, 2002).

Adults who were raised in strict households—especially with authoritarian fathers—are more likely to procrastinate. This may be due to fear of failure, or due to the satisfaction of rebellion as an adult when no longer obligated to follow the authoritarian's rules.

Consider: Were you raised in a particularly strict household? Do you get a sense of satisfaction from knowing you have the right and authority to delay tasks if you want to?

All or nothing mindset

> *Carl weighs in at 362lbs. He's got to lose about 200lbs to be a healthy weight.*

*What're the chances of him ever
getting that done?*

*He's never going to reach his target
weight, so he can't find the
motivation to lose any weight at all.*

Procrastinators with an 'all or nothing'
mentality often fail to get started on tasks
because they can't see the light at the end
of the tunnel. They do not see the point in
starting a task if they're never going to
reach their end goal (Judith Belmont,
2011).

Consider: Have you been putting off a task
because you can't see yourself ever
completing it? Do you think if you can't
reach your final goal there's no point in
working towards it at all?

Disassociation from future self

*Tom stretches and sits back with a
smile on his face. He could work on
his thesis...but he'll do it next week.*

Many procrastinators will put off what they can do
today because their 'future self' can do it tomorrow.

A lack of self-continuity means that people who
procrastinate in this way do not envisage how the

burden of this task or how the failure to complete a task may affect their future self (Timothy A. Pychyl E.-M. C.-H., 2015).

They see no consequences to delaying a task because they have confidence that their future self will carry the burden.

Consider: Do you often allow your future self to carry the burden of tasks you could complete today?

Conclusion

Most people understand procrastination as a symptom of laziness but as we can see from this chapter, the reasons for procrastination are often much more complex.

Throughout this chapter, you've been asked to consider the reasons why you personally procrastinate. Keep a note of these reasons so that you can identify the best ways to fight your personal procrastination demons as we go through this book.

Now we understand some of the major causes of procrastination, we'll look through some tools and practical ways to overcome it.

Combatting Partial Naivete

Pre-Commitment and partial naivete

Pre-commitment is the act of committing to completing an act at a dedicated time in the future. In laymen's terms, it is committing to a scheduled task.

Pre-commitment is the procrastinator's nemesis, especially for those procrastinators who are a victim to the trait of partial naivete.

Let's remind ourselves of Chloe's case study in Chapter Three.

> *Chloe happily works on her company's social media pages. It's her favorite part of the job. She loves creating posts and replying to all the comments. It's easy and fun.*
>
> *She glances at the clock. It's 3pm and she must have that accounts report completed by 5pm.*
>
> *She's great at reports. They only take twenty minutes, tops. She'll come back to it in an hour or so and have plenty of time to get it done.*

Chloe has committed to beginning her task at 4pm. She's fallen victim to the habit of partial naivete.

Let's look at three different examples of how this could go wrong:

1) *Chloe waits until 4pm to begin the task. At 4.10pm, her boss calls her in for a meeting. She tells her there is an emergency and she needs all hands on deck for the rest of the day. Chloe now has no time to complete the accounts report and will look unprofessional in tomorrow's meeting unless she takes her work home to complete.*

2) *Chloe begins the task at 4pm and immediately finds that a large chunk of information is missing. She quickly runs to the Sales Department to get the missing data but is told that the person she needs to speak to has left early for a doctor's appointment.*

3) *Chloe begins the task at 4pm, expecting it to take around twenty minutes, as usual. However, what she didn't anticipate was the sheer volume of errors that she'd find in this particular report. It will take hours to trace the root of the errors and she's only left herself with one hour to do it all.*

These examples show the problem with partial naivete. Procrastinating because you believe you will have time to complete a task is trying to predict the future. You can't account for what problems you'll run into or what will change.

The benefits of playing it safe

So, how would things have gone differently if Chloe had started the task at the beginning of the day?

Let's take a look at how things could have been.

1) *Chloe waits until 4pm to begin the task. At 4.10pm, her boss calls her in for a meeting. She tells her there is an emergency and she needs all hands on deck for the rest of the day. Fortunately for Chloe, she started her accounts report this afternoon and are on the closing statement. She can finish in the next five minutes and be available to her boss for the rest of the day.*

2) *Chloe begins the task at 4pm and immediately finds that a large chunk of information is missing. She quickly runs to the Sales Department to get the missing data but is told that the person she needs to speak to has left early for a doctor's appointment. Luckily, it's only 2pm. Chloe has time to speak to a different member of staff to ask for their help. Together, they're able to trace the missing information and Chloe still has time to complete her report before the end of the day.*

3) *Chloe begins the task at 4pm, expecting it to take around twenty minutes, as usual. However, what she didn't anticipate was the sheer volume of errors that she'd find in this particular report.*

Chloe is frustrated. She knows she won't get this completed today. However, as she's caught the issue early, it does give her time to go to her boss and explain the situation. Her boss assigns another member of staff to help Chloe, and together, they make great progress.

As we can see from these examples, it was Chloe's procrastination that leads to her failure in all three scenarios.

However, telling Chloe simply to not procrastinate is not particularly helpful.

So, what are some practical steps Chloe could have taken to avoid the consequences of partial naivete?

Combatting partial naivete: Practical steps

Let's take a look at some practical steps that can be taken to avoid falling into the trap of partial naivete.

In short, the solution is easy: Play it safe.

1) Always assume the worst.

When judging how long a task will take, make the judgment on the basis that everything goes wrong. Assume your document is full of errors, your computer crashes, and you have a terrible migraine.

Leave twice as long as you need for any given task, or longer if you can. The more time you have to complete a task, the more opportunity you have to overcome unforeseen obstacles.

Even if you've done the same task a hundred times before, don't assume that everything will go to plan this time.

Consider whether a task is an important one. If the answer is yes, abide by this rule: Assume the worst and leave at least twice as long as you need to complete the task.

2) Realize that you cannot and do not control all variables

Those who suffer from partial naivety do so because they believe everything will go to plan and be as simple as it has been previously. They rely on their own abilities and time management.

However, it is essential for this type of procrastinator to realize that there will always be factors outside of their control.

Imagine a different scenario: You have to catch a plane at 3pm.

You are not the pilot. You do not decide when the plane takes off. If you are not there on time, the plane will leave without you. The consequences of this are that you will miss your flight, possibly miss a connection, and waste money on airfare and a hotel you never arrived at.

To combat partial naivete, you need to be aware that variables may arise that are outside of your control. In fact, the only control you have is to have the foresight to avoid a last-minute rush.

Give yourself plenty of time, anticipate obstacles, and tackle tasks calmly.

3) Save the best for last

Chloe used the excuse of working on social media to put off the more important task of completing the accounts report.

We all have favorite parts of our jobs or study, but unless these are the priority, they should never be an excuse.

Save these fun parts as a reward for a job well done when the important tasks are complete.

4) Be self-aware

Chloe put off her main task because she trusts her future self to have self-control. However, if she is putting off the task now, why does she trust her future self to complete the task?

A certain amount of self-awareness can change a partially naïve person into what is known as a sophisticated thinker—a person who is self-aware of their issues with self-control.

Do not give your future self the benefit of the doubt. Make the assumption your future self is tired, hungry, upset, or not in the mood.

The present you are sitting at a desk, completely capable of doing this task. Be self-aware of this fact, and use it to harness a sense of discipline.

5) Consider discipline now vs. discipline later

The previous point spoke about putting trust in our future selves.

Our future self is the same person as the present self; the present you who is putting off that task.

Understand that your future self is also a procrastinator. You will not have a magical change of personality if you put off a task until later. However, what you will do is create greater stress, worry, and time pressure by delaying what needs to be done.

When you understand that nothing will change within you by 'later', you are left with the fact that getting this done *now* is simply a matter of discipline.

The workplace method

Traditionally, procrastinators do not respond well to plans because the issue is not time management. The tendency to procrastinate has a deeper cause.

However, if you are a procrastinator who suffers from

the curse of partial naivete, then this chapter should have sparked some self-recognition that will help you complete the following tasks.

1) Identify your main priority
2) Estimate how long this task will take based on previous experience
3) Double that timeframe
4) Start an hour earlier than your new figure
5) Reward yourself with your favorite tasks if you have remaining time.

For example: *Chloe estimates the accounts report will take 20 mins.*
2 x 20 minutes = 40 minutes

40 minutes + 1 hour = 1h 40m.

So, if Chloe must have this task complete by 5pm, her very latest start time will be 3.20pm.

This method works very well for work-based tasks where all duties must be completed within the working day.

Of course, the earlier you begin a task, the better. However, procrastinators are infamous for leaving the worst until last.

This method will minimize the likelihood of running into obstacles. Practice this formula with each new work task until leaving yourself plenty of time to complete a task becomes second nature

Overcoming the fear of failure
Procrastination and the fear of failure

Many procrastinators put off important tasks that need to be done because they're afraid what they do won't be good enough.

Often, these procrastinators will occupy themselves with the minutiae of the task. They may get everything prepared without ever actually getting started on the main part of the task.

Let's remind ourselves of Miguel's struggle:

> *Miguel is a struggling college student who is just getting by with his grades. He has an essay to complete and he just can't get started. If his past grades are anything to go by, this essay is doomed to fail.*
>
> *Every time he thinks about starting, he feels sick. This feeling of dread takes over and even though he knows how important the assignment is, he finds himself burying his head in the sand.*

Miguel's fear of failure is based on his past experience of getting bad grades.

So what can Miguel do to overcome these fears?

<u>Practical steps for overcoming the fear of failure</u>

1) Find the benefits of past failures

Tchiki Davis, Berkeley Graduate, and well-being-technology expert advises that finding the benefits of past failures can help to overcome the fear of future failure (Davis, 2018).

A simple, practical task she advises for this purpose is to list the positive outcomes of past failures.

Let's use Miguel as an example:

- *When Miguel failed his previous exam, his professor guided him to new resources which were invaluable to him throughout the rest of his course*

- *Miguel was marked down on an essay for failing to properly cite his references. Now he makes sure every quote is cited and a full bibliography is always included in his assignments. This has elevated the quality of his work.*

- *When Miguel found himself struggling with his physics course, he made the choice to switch to biology. He has found he loves biology and is thriving in that particular course.*

Although Miguel experienced failure in previous assignments, there were positive outcomes from those experiences. He found new resources, improved how he does his work, and found a new subject he enjoys more and finds success in.

The point is, you either win or you learn.

'Failure' is a blanket term which undermines the positive outcomes that are inherent in every experience.

No matter how terribly a situation seems to have unfolded, there is always a lesson learned that decreases the likelihood of future failure.

Make your own list of positive outcomes from past failures and consider what the positive outcomes might be for your current task even if the outcome doesn't go as planned.

2) Foresee obstacles

The fact is you may very well run into obstacles in a task.

Visualizing these obstacles in advance gives you the opportunity to mentally prepare yourself for them and to make contingency plans.

Let's use Miguel again as an example.

He knows he's going to struggle with the essay. Why?

He might think he'll get writer's block, that he won't be able to find good sources to cite, or that he won't understand the material.

Whether Miguel does the task now or later, these obstacles will remain a possibility.

A 2011 study in the *Journal of Experimental Psychology* (Heather Barry Kappes, 2011) found that those who practiced positive thinking—imagining all that might go well in the week ahead—were more likely to achieve poorly in comparison to those who foresaw and visualized likely obstacles. This is because those who foresaw obstacles generated more energy for the task, knowing there would be issues to face.

You are more likely to perform well if you have realistic expectations of the difficulty of the task, so take time to visualize obstacles as a means of talking yourself out of procrastination.

3) Avoid anxiety triggers until after the task is complete

> *Miguel is about to start writing his essay but decides to check his emails first. Sitting there in his inbox is the email from his professor reminding him that if he doesn't get 60% on his next essay, he will have to repeat the semester. Miguel's stomach knots up.*

Miguel had managed to get himself in the mindset to

work on his essay but became demotivated when the email reinforced his fear of failure.

> Think about the task you're putting off. What factors, things, or people might reinforce your fear of failure surrounding this task?

Give yourself time and space away from these triggers until the task is complete to help stay in control of your fear.

4) Talk it out

Many people who fear failure mistakenly believe they are the only ones who are struggling.

The truth is, almost everyone feels pressure in some form or another.

Talking about your fear with a friend, colleague, spouse or peer can help to assuage them and let you realize that you're not the only person who worries.

Use this method as a means to get your mind into a calmer state so that you can concentrate on the task at hand.

5) Exposure

The first time you do anything new, it can be scary.

A first date, the first time flying, the first time trying to speak to someone in a foreign language...

However, fear dissipates when we do these things again and again. The serial dater or the person who found 'the one' isn't fearful, neither is the frequent flyer or the English-speaker who has muddled along for long enough in a new country.

The point is, exposure to what we fear is one of the best ways to overcome that fear.

When the unknown becomes known, we no longer have to be afraid.

Developing discipline

Approximately 18% of procrastinators have no good reason for why they put tasks off. Simply, they lack the willpower to commit to a task.

Many procrastinators will blame a lack of motivation for why they don't get things done. However, motivation is a myth. It is an idealized mood or urges that people expect to come upon them to generate willpower spontaneously.

The fact is, willpower is an act of discipline—and discipline can be developed. However, it is a learned behavior.

Here are some ways you can learn to practice self-discipline and defeat procrastination.

Practical steps to developing discipline

1) Confront discomfort

You're putting off that task because you know you won't enjoy doing it.

The fact is, some tasks are unpleasant, boring, or frustrating to do. The only way to get on with the task is to accept that you are going to be bored or frustrated.

You have to implement some tough self-love and set yourself strict boundaries.

2) Know your temptations

What is it that prevents you from doing that important, albeit dull task? Netflix, Facebook, a phone call with your best friend?

The temptation is the nemesis of self-discipline. Remove temptations from your environment to make it easier to focus.

3) Make productivity habit

Habit is the cornerstone of discipline.

Schedule your time so that the most important tasks are completed at the same time daily.

Imagine you are an aspiring writer; you could ensure you write for an hour before work every day.

Habits seem difficult to implement, but the fact is, we are all creatures of habit. We all complete the same tasks day in, day out, without recognizing them as acts of discipline and habit.

For example, every day most of us will prepare and eat our meals, shower, brush our teeth, and comb our hair. We don't think of these things as chores because they are part of our daily routine.

Make those tasks you're putting off part of your own routine and stick to that routine rigidly. This is the only way to create a habit.

4) Set clear goals with measurable targets

Unclear goals are an easy excuse to only put in a fraction of the effort you could.

Compare these two goals set for a writer:

- "Do some writing today"
- "Write 3,000 words by 12pm"

The first goal is flexible and easy to satisfy with minimal effort. A person with this goal could write a single paragraph and claim they met their goal.

On the other hand, the second goal is clear, concise and sets a measurable target.

Make sure that your own targets have measurable results and be strict with yourself that you won't stray from the task until you have met the minimum target you have set for yourself.

5) Make yourself accountable

Hold yourself accountable to someone in your support network, whether that be a spouse, friend, peer or colleague.

For example, share your daily goals with a partner and ask them to check in with you at the end of the day.

This extra layer of accountability means you can't hide your lack of effort from someone.

And if you're being really strict with yourself, don't allow your partner to take your word for it.

They should see your progress in its physical form, whether that is a completed essay, document or other evidence that you have done what you set out to do.

6) Recognize your 'zone'

When are you at your most focused? When do you have the fewest distractions? When do you feel most calm? When do you have the best resources?

Consider what times, places, people, and resources best inspire and motivate you and schedule yourself to complete tasks at these times under those conditions.

In a work environment or other already-structured day, think of your day as a series of segments. Which segments are your most productive?

For example, a morning person may be most productive between 9:00-12:00, while other people work best in the calm of the evening.

Perhaps the hour before lunch is your prime time, knowing you will get a lunch break as a 'reward'.

Figure out when you work at your best and schedule your priority tasks for then.

Becoming Independent
The downfalls of dependency

An unhealthy dependency on others slows us down, puts pressure on those around us, and undermines our confidence in ourselves. We can never reach our true potential if we wait for others to step in when things get hard.

Read the following list of traits. How many of these statements ring true for you?

- If I wait long enough, someone else will step in to help or do it for me
- There are so many things I'm not capable of doing myself
- Someone else will do it better
- I need reassurance that my decisions are the right ones
- I don't like taking responsibility for important tasks and decisions
- I get into a tailspin when I spend too long working alone
- I feel more motivated when I'm part of a team.

If these are mantras you often find playing out in your head, then it is likely your tendency to procrastinate stems from an unhealthy dependence on others and a lack of faith in your own abilities.

So, how can we break the cycle of unhealthy dependency in our work and personal lives?

Case study

Let's remember Laura from Chapter Three.

> *Laura hangs around by her colleague's desk hopefully.*
>
> *"Have you done your bit on the Excel report yet?" She asks.*
>
> *Robin rolls his eyes. He's used to Laura's hinting. "I can't help you right now, Laura. I'm up to my eyeballs in my own work."*
>
> *"Could you just show me how to insert that formula again?"*
>
> *"Fine. Sit down and I'll show you."*

Laura may not realize that her dependency on others is causing problems in the workplace. She is distracting others while hindering herself. She will never progress in the workplace if she can't complete tasks independently.

What could Laura have done differently?

Let's take a look at an alternate scenario.

> *Laura starts working on her Excel report and realizes she doesn't know how to insert a formula. She feels a fleeting*

*sense of panic but then decides to push
through. She fires up her internet
browser and searches how to insert the
formula. After reading a few how-tos
and watching a couple of YouTube
tutorials, she understands how to insert
the formula. She's proud of herself and
has learned a new skill that will make
her work easier in the future.*

In the first scenario, Laura's kneejerk reaction was to
rely on a colleague to help her. In the second scenario,
Laura took steps to help herself. This is how self-
reliance is developed; certainly, you will face obstacles
you've never faced before during your work or personal
life, but the art of self-reliance is trusting yourself to be
able to find a solution, even if you're encountering an
issue for the first time.

Practical steps to developing self-reliance

1) Accept responsibility

Face your fears and accept that you are responsible
for your own actions, the way you complete tasks,
and the outcome of your own work. You will get
credit for a job well done and you will face the
consequences of your own errors.

For some people, this idea is terrifying, but learning
to be accountable is key to breaking free from the
cycle of unhealthy dependency, and consequently

avoiding procrastination by waiting for others to step in.

2) Develop a skills bank

Consider every experience a learning opportunity and take responsibility for building your own skills and resource banks.

When someone shows you how to do something new, write it down.

When you make a new contact, keep a record.

If you don't know how to do something, research it, and find a way to retain that information.

Become a sponge instead of a sieve. The more skills you have under your belt, the more tasks you can tackle, and the less dependent you will become.

3) Have personal goals

Ambition can drive the desire to be self-reliant. If you want that promotion, you'll have to earn it. If you want your relationship with your partner to improve, you have to put in the work.

Having no end goal in sight can create complacency. If we take no pride in our work or have no ultimate target in mind, there is no reason to strive.

This can lead to procrastination and reliance on others to do things for you.

Consider how your actions will affect your work life, personal life, or relationships positively and take steps to make those changes happen.

4) Create your own benchmarks for success

Let's look at a new case study.

Bryan recently passed his driving test but hasn't done much driving since he got his license. One morning he finds his mother stressed because she's run out of her medication. Proudly, Bryan drives a completely new route into the city to the pharmacy to get them for her.

When he returns, she asks him whether he organized a repeat prescription for next month. He tells her no.

She sighs impatiently. "I wish you'd just waited an hour. I would have done it myself."

By driving to the pharmacy, Bryan was exercising a newfound sense of independence. He relied on himself to complete the chore of getting his mother's medication. However, because he failed to organize the repeat prescription, he's been left feeling deflated and like he's failed. Next time, he won't go himself.

The problem here is that Bryan's achievement has been overshadowed by his failure to organize a repeat prescription. The result is that he now doubts his own ability to complete the task independently and has become demotivated by someone else's reaction.

Events like this happen all the time in the workplace and in our personal lives. Our own achievements are constantly undermined by others. However, we must learn to judge our successes by our own benchmarks.

The fact is, Bryan drove a new route without issue. He exercised his independence and was right to rely on himself—he safely completed the journey.

If you are going to rely on yourself, you must also be kind to yourself. Recognize your successes and have compassion for yourself when you make mistakes.

You are capable of achieving things independently, and any error in those achievements should not detract from the success of the achievement itself.

5) Manipulate yourself, not others

A dependent person uses others' abilities and generosity to their own advantage. They are quite willing to let others step in and take over for them, to complete tasks they are capable of completing themselves, and to allow others' giving natures to be used for their own benefit.

One of the keys to becoming self-reliant is to recognize that this behavior is manipulative. Instead of manipulating others, we must learn to manipulate ourselves.

What must you say to yourself to convince yourself to complete the task; to face the obstacle?

Next time you think about letting someone else do something you could do yourself, ask yourself the following questions.

- Am I capable of doing this myself?
- Do I have something more important to be doing?
- What are the benefits of doing this myself?
- How will I reward myself if I complete this task?

These questions encourage you to manipulate your own manner of thinking; questioning 'Why *not* me?'.

6) Recognize your strengths and successes

Visualize the task you are facing. What similar tasks or situations have you faced in the past? How did you tackle them? What did you learn from these experiences? What did you do well? What are your own skills?

Bring whatever you're good at into your current task. It will build your confidence to know part of what you've done encompasses your best strengths.

For example:

- James doesn't want to write his resume, but he's great at graphic design. He makes his formatting top-notch and feels more pride and confidence in the end result.
- Susan is terrible at writing reports but great at public speaking. She asks if she can go through her report verbally with her boss. This gives her the chance to explain out loud anything her boss doesn't understand. She goes back later and makes those changes in the hard copy.

Just remember—don't let this turn into another excuse to procrastinate.

Overcoming anxiety

The state of anxiety

"You know that feeling when you're rocking on the back legs of your chair and suddenly for just a split second you think you're about to fall; that feeling in your chest? Imagine that split second feeling being frozen in time and lodged in your chest for minutes/hours/days, and imagine with it that sense of impending doom and dread sticking around too, but sometimes you don't even know why."

(Wilkinson, 2017)

This is what it feels like to be in a state of anxiety. For many procrastinators, putting off important tasks is far more about avoiding this state of anxiety than avoiding the task itself.

A vicious cycle

It is also important to be aware of the fact that avoiding tasks that make us anxious—procrastinating—only creates a vicious cycle. We avoid a task because we are anxious, and then become more anxious as the task becomes more pressing.

Let's remind ourselves of what Hilary from Chapter Three was facing:

> *Hilary has to finish filling out her divorce forms but hasn't got around to it. She*

*knows that when she begins, it's all
going to come rushing back—the
feelings of worthlessness, the memories
of her husband cheating, the panic
about how to divide up their
possessions...As long as she doesn't
think about the divorce, she can
function. She just can't handle it right
now.*

Hilary is avoiding the task because of her fear of
stepping into that state of anxiety, even though filling in
those divorce papers is a crucial step in freeing herself
from the emotional trap she is in and moving on.

Many of us procrastinate for the same reason, and the
way to get through it is to practice proper self-care
while approaching the task ahead.

How to face the state of anxiety

Anxiety sufferers can employ the following coping
mechanisms to help them face their anxiety:

- Take time out—listen to music, practice
  relaxation techniques, etc.

  Leave yourself enough time for a task that you
  can intersperse your work with small 'time-outs'
  to help you manage your anxiety around the
  task. Make sure you schedule and limit these
  'time-outs' as far as possible. Make them part of

your work process rather than distractions from it.

- Limit alcohol and caffeine

  Alcohol and caffeine can act as triggers for anxiety. Instead, drink water and other non-caffeinated beverages.

- Do your best

  Perfection isn't always possible. Accept that your best is all you can do, no matter the outcome.

- Replace negative thoughts with positive ones

  Retrain your inner voice to be kinder and replace negative thoughts with positive ones. For example, when a thought occurs such as 'I can't do this', force yourself to replace it with a positive mantra: 'I *can* do this".

- Talk to someone

  Communicate your struggles with friends, family, colleagues, or peers. The proper support network can give us confidence that we are capable of completing a task or that we will be able to cope if things don't go to plan.

(Mental Health America)

Seek support

There is no 'one size fits all' cure for procrastination. In earlier chapters, we've discussed the importance of self-reliance. In this chapter, we will discuss the importance of seeking support.

For the anxious procrastinator, a lack of willpower or discipline is not the issue—fear is the issue.

In these cases, seeking support or even delegating aspects of your tasks can be key to moving forward.

Let's look at how Hilary could have sought support.

> *Hilary sits at the table surrounded by all the papers. She has come to the part where she has to fill out her bid for child custody. She remembers how her partner left her—and her children—for another woman and breaks down at the thought of losing them too.*
>
> *Her cell rings. It's her mother.*
>
> *"Hilary, what's wrong?"*
>
> *"I'm working on these divorce papers and I can't do it. I keep thinking about the hell he put us through and can't stop crying. If I don't get these in by the end of the week, I'm going*

to risk him getting temporary custody of the kids."

"I'm coming over," her mother says. "Put the kettle on. I'll take a read through the paperwork and we'll see if we can figure it out together."

Once Hilary's mother arrives, she feels calmer. She's able to let her mother do the reading and interpreting the difficult legal jargon. Her mother then rephrases the document into simple questions that Hilary can answer while her mother completes the form. When she cries, her mother comforts her and then gently refocuses her attention to the task at hand.

The anxious procrastinator does not need to feel guilty if they cannot complete a task alone.

The delegation, peer support, and working alongside someone else are key resources in the anxious procrastinator's toolbox.

Reframe your perspective

1. You're putting off doing your tax return because you know you can't afford the payment.
2. You haven't made arrangements for your brother's funeral because it's too upsetting.

3. *You haven't picked up your belongings from your ex's house because you know it will cause another argument.*

In these situations, it is dread and the fear of entering that state of anxiety that is preventing progress.

Reframing is the art of putting a positive spin on a negative thought.

For example:

1. *Once I've done my tax return, I'll know what repayment plans I'm eligible for and can start to get my finances in order.*
2. *Arranging a respectful and loving funeral will be the best tribute I can pay my brother.*
3. *Getting my belongings will close the door on a relationship I'm ready to move on from. It's the closure I need to rebuild my life.*

Practicing the art of reframing can help you to find the inner strength to face a difficult situation or task you've been putting off. This practice reminds you why the task is important and what benefits you will gain from getting it done—even if the whole situation seems like a negative one.

What is your perspective on the current situation you're facing? How can you reframe it into a more positive one?

Making hot and cold work for you
The hot-cold empathy gap: a deeper look

Let's revisit the hot-cold empathy gap briefly described in Chapter Three.

In short, the hot-cold empathy gap describes our habit of assuming we will have willpower in a future state.

Often, we make decisions about our schedule and activities at a time when we are feeling focused and calm. We do this under the false assumption that we will be in the same state of mind when the times comes to undertake the scheduled task.

Let's remind ourselves of Liam's struggle:

> *Liam just found out the money his best friend borrowed to 'pay for his dog's medicine' was actually used to buy a new games console. He's furious.*
>
> *Despite how angry Liam is, he's got an exam to study for. He puts it off. There's no way he could study when he's feeling this mad.*

In this situation, Liam has planned to study while he is in a 'cold' state—calm and focused. However, when the time comes to study, he finds himself in a 'hot' state due to anger he wasn't able to predict.

Liam's story is a good representation of the hot-cold empathy gap.

Temptation

The temptation is another obstacle that procrastinator's face—especially those that procrastinate due to this hot-cold empathy gap.

Let's take a look at a new case study.

> *Gary's wife gets furious with him when he spends too much gambling. It has caused countless arguments in their marriage and unnecessary financial problems.*
>
> *She doesn't know it, but tonight he's going out with his buddies to a casino. He was hesitant when he was first invited, but reasoned to himself that he would only take fifty dollars and wouldn't spend a cent more. With this resolve in mind, he went to the casino.*
>
> *However, once he was there, he got caught up in the excitement of the casino. One of his friends had a big win and it spurred him on to try his own luck. The adrenalin, the alcohol, and the enjoyment he gets from gambling soon turn that fifty dollars spends into a two-hundred dollar spend.*
>
> *The next morning, Gary is filled with a sense of*

dread. He's blown two-hundred dollars he didn't have to spare and his wife will be rightfully upset with him.

Why did he agree to go?

Gary made the classic mistake that is the basis of the hot-cold empathy gap—in a calm and collected state of mind, he made the assumption that he would have the willpower to resist temptation in the future.

The same principle applies to chronic procrastinators. They put tasks off to the future because they make the assumption that they will have the willpower to resist the temptation of a better offer later, that they won't get distracted, and that they'll have full focus when the time comes to knuckle down.

Here are some classic examples of scenarios this type of procrastinator finds themselves in:

> *Judy made the decision that she would fill in the application for her internship at the end of the day. She's occupied herself with other things all afternoon and has only just sat down at her desk as it's nearing 7pm. Just as she's getting stuck in, her roommate comes in.*
>
> *"Judy! Are you coming out with us*

tonight?"

"I can't. I've got to finish this application."

Her roommate scoffs. "You can do it tomorrow."

Judy knows she's got other things on tomorrow, but she can't resist the lure of a good night out. She closes her laptops and smiles. She'll do it tomorrow.

***

Harry promised himself he would finish his project before setting off on holiday for the week. He carved out a couple of hours on Friday before his flight to get it done.

However, when it comes time to finish his project off, he finds himself worrying about whether he's ready for the holiday. Has he packed his passport? He forgot to exchange his currency!

The flight is leaving in a few hours. He has to make sure he's *ready. He tells himself he'll finish his project on the plane.*

***

Mary is meant to be on a diet. She did a food shop at the beginning of the week and made sure she had plenty of fresh fruit and veg with every intention of cooking a healthy home-cooked meal after work. However, by the time she gets in, she's exhausted. She's been on her feet all day, the phone was ringing off the hook, and her boss was being a jerk. She simply doesn't have the energy to cook right now. She grabs a frozen pizza from the freezer. One cheat day won't hurt. She'll start her diet again tomorrow.

All three of these people have the same thing in common—they've put off a scheduled task until later. They've procrastinated. Again.

All three of them made an attempt at time-management. They all had the best intentions. They'd all considered their priorities and made plans.

However, when the time came, all three found reasons not to go through with their scheduled tasks.

This is the hallmark of a procrastinator afflicted by the hot-cold empathy gap.

So, how can we overcome this tendency?

Resisting temptation

The hot-cold procrastinator must resist temptation.

There are things that can be done to assist this. For example, the procrastinator can remove distractions and temptations from their immediate environment.

However, sometimes it is impossible to predict what temptations will present themselves. In these instances, the only possible solution is to exercise self-control.

Let's take another look at Judy. What would have happened if she'd exercised greater self-control?

> Judy made the decision that she would fill in the application for her internship at the end of the day. She's occupied herself with other things all afternoon and has only just sat down at her desk as it's nearing 7pm. Just as she's getting stuck in, her roommate comes in.
>
> "Judy! Are you coming out with us tonight?"
>
> "I can't. I've got to finish this application."
>
> Her roommate scoffs. "You can do it tomorrow."
>
> "I'd love to, but I'm serious. I can't come out

tonight."

In this altered scenario, Judy completes her application and exercised self-control to avoid further procrastination.

Like a discipline, self-control is a skill that can be learned.

The Marshmallow Test

Self-control often fails us when we put immediate gratification before our long-term goals.

In Judy's case, the temptation of a great night out trumps the importance of completing her application.

Learning how to delay gratification to achieve a more important goal and reap a greater reward is the cornerstone to developing self-control.

Let's take a look at The Stanford Marshmallow Experiment to visualize this habit better.

The Stanford Marshmallow Experiment

In the late 60s and early 70s, psychologist Walter Mischel led a series of experiments to study the conditions that promote the delay of gratification.

The test involved children who were given two options:

a) To eat a small treat immediately
b) To wait for a larger treat

The purpose of the experiment was to discover under which conditions the children were best able to resist the temptation to take the small treat immediately, thereby experiencing immediate gratification, and to instead wait to receive the bigger treat.

The results of the experiment have been used to understand the psychology of immediate vs. delayed gratification.

(Conti, 2019)

Judy opted for immediate gratification, i.e. 'the small treat' of a night out instead of the big pay-off of a potential internship.

So, what did the marshmallow test teach psychologists about how we can delay gratification for greater rewards?

The Hot-and-Cool-Model

The psychologists found that how the reward was visualized played a large role in whether the child was able to hold out for the bigger treat or not.

Children who were told to think of the marshmallow as a 'fluffy cloud' were able to wait longer than those who were told to think of how good it tasted.

The feeling of temptation for immediate gratification is referred to as a 'hot mode', and the ability to think of the greater reward is thought of as the 'cold mode'.

Children who were able to activate their cold mode were better waiters than those children who got stuck in hot mode and could only think of how tasty the marshmallow would be.

If we apply this to Judy's case, we'll see that when she's presented with the option of a fun night out, she goes into hot mode—all she can think about is the immediate pleasure of drinking and dancing with her friends.

If she were to activate her cold mode, she'd instead think about the importance of the task at hand. The application is the 'fluffy cloud' while the night out is the delicious treat.

However, we can't fully blame Judy for her lack of self-control. The study also found that stress impaired the ability to delay gratification. So, for somebody putting all their eggs in one basket, so to speak, the stress could be immense.

Judy has several ways to combat her issues with self-control:

- Learn adaptive reasoning, i.e. how to switch on her 'cool mode' and learn how to think of the immediate pleasure as a small reward and the completion of the task as a greater reward worth waiting for
- Identify and manager her stressors – as stress activates the 'hot mode', Judy will have more success if she's as relaxed as possible. Drinking plenty of water, choosing a calm environment, and leaving plenty of time to complete the task at hand can all help her to succeed and avoid the temptation to procrastinate.

Next time you are procrastinating, practice activating your own cool mode. Ask yourself whether the short-term gratification of an immediate pleasure really outweighs the value of what you're putting off.

Overcoming FOMO (the fear of missing out)

'FOMO'—the fear of missing out—was officially added to the Oxford English dictionary in 2013. The fear that by doing one thing we are going to miss out on something better is a sensation we're all familiar with, and to the chronic procrastinator, it's a nightmare.

A 2013 study published by Elsevier defines it as:

"the uneasy and sometimes all-consuming feeling that you're missing out – that your peers are doing, in the know about, or in possession of more or something better than you". Under this framing of FoMO, nearly three-quarters of young adults reported they experienced the phenomenon."

(Andrew K. Przybylski, July 2013)

Overcoming FOMO is key to a procrastinator focusing on the task at hand and using their scheduled time as they intended.

So, what are some methods of overcoming the fear of missing out?

1) Avoid digital communications and social media

Texting and social media are poison to FOMO-ers. When everyone seems to be having a good time and photos are popping up of all your friends laughing and joking, it makes you feel isolated and miserable.

The solution is not to join in, but rather to disconnect from digital media for a while. Turn of your cell, log out of your social media and be in the zone. The less you know about what everyone else is up to, the less you'll feel left out and the greater focus you'll be able to generate on the task at hand.

2) See the difference between what is fun and what is important

A simple practice to help you overcome the fear of missing out is to ask yourself what you'll be missing out on if you *don't* do what you're supposed to be doing.

For example, Judy may miss out on a great night of partying if she stays in, but if she doesn't complete her application, she may miss out on an internship. What is really the greater loss?

3) Make social events part of your calendar

...Or time for hobbies, or that TV show, or whatever it is you're scared of missing out on.

Schedule in time for the things you enjoy alongside those tasks you know you *must* do.

Judy might not be able to join in on the night she needs to do her application, but there is no reason she can't arrange a night out the following week, or have lunch with her friends the next day.

Knowing that good times are scheduled in can help alleviate the feeling that you're stuck in a hole doing something you really don't want to be doing at all.

Preloading decisions

Preloading decisions is a term used to describe

decisions that are made in a cold state in preparation for a hot state.

Basically, if you know you may be presented with temptations when attempting to tackle an important task, preloading decisions allows you to decide how you are going to combat those temptations while you are in a cold state.

Let's use Mary as an example.

She's on a diet and in her given scenario, she ends up giving in to temptation and eating a pizza when she finds herself tired at the end of the day, putting off her healthy eating kick until the next day.

If Mary had preloaded her decisions, they may have looked something like this:

- If I'm tired when I get home, I will pick up a pre-made salad from the corner shop
- If I don't want to cook something complicated when I get home, I will microwave a jacket potato and have it with a simple filling like baked beans or tuna
- If I don't want to cook when I get home, I'll eat the pizza, but only within my allowed calorie intake for the day, i.e. two slices instead of the whole pizza.

In this instance, Mary hasn't fallen victim to the hot-cold empathy gap. She has predicted her lack of willpower and made contingency plans for that eventuality.

Think about a task you have put off. What obstacles or temptations are likely to arise that will stop you from sticking to your plan and getting this task done?

Make a list of preloaded decisions to plan how you will avoid giving in.

Capitalize on your cold states

Recognize when you are in a cold state and use this to your advantage.

If you wake up in a good mood—tackle the task.

If you're feeling super motivated—tackle the task.

If you're unusually focused—tackle the task.

If the house is unexpectedly quiet—tackle the task.

Procrastinators make plans to do tasks later assuming that everything will work out perfectly; they'll be in a great mood, they'll have the time, there will be no distractions. However, to avoid the consequences of things going wrong, you have to be willing to change your plan if the optimal conditions present themselves before the scheduled time.

Becoming accountable to yourself

Remember Lucy?

> *Lucy doesn't know why she*
> *procrastinates; all she knows is that*
> *she feels satisfied when she does. It*
> *feels good to control your own*
> *schedule, doesn't it? She's a grown*
> *woman. If she wants to sit and watch*
> *Netflix instead of writing that*
> *dissertation, that's her call.*

Lucy reveals in her own authority. She's a grown woman, in her own home, in control of her own life. It feels good to be able to put something off she doesn't feel like doing.

Unfortunately, the sad fact is that Lucy isn't in control. She's constantly putting off important tasks and suffering the consequences of her procrastination.

She's constantly under pressure, tired, irritable and snapping at her boyfriend. In the moment of choosing an hour of TV over an hour of work, she feels satisfied with her decision, but when she next looks at the clock and sees how much time she's wasted, she feels awful about all that wasted time.

Lucy has always been accountable to someone.

Her parents, teachers, and partners have always had extremely high expectations of her and she ended up developing the urge to dig her heels in and just *stop*. She wants to decide for herself when to work and when to rest.

The problem is, she seems to hardly ever end up making the right choice.

She used to be so productive. Why can't she get anything done anymore?

***

Lucy has always been accountable to others and has enjoyed the freedom of being accountable to nobody but herself. The problem is, when she's her own authority, she lets herself off easily every time. She becomes complacent. She rewards herself often, takes lots of breaks, and constantly procrastinates.

She needs to become accountable to herself and exercise her authority to force herself to reach her full potential.

How can she achieve this?

Developing personal accountability

Lucy was always able to do well when she was accountable to someone else, but now she needs to be accountable to herself. She needs to develop a sense of personal accountability.

If you are a procrastinator who enjoys the freedom of

only being accountable to yourself and end up failing to hold yourself to the high standards you wish you could, then you also need to learn how to develop this skill.

Here are a few methods for developing personal accountability:

1) Be honest with yourself

When we don't have a high level of personal accountability, it's easy to firstly blame other people or things for our lack of success. It's also easy to make excuses for yourself.

Show yourself some tough love next time you find yourself procrastinating. Is whatever is distracting you or causing you to delay honestly worth putting off the task? Is the delay genuinely the fault of circumstances outside your control, or was putting the task off a choice?

2) Don't overcommit

If you've got too much on your plate, something is bound to get pushed back.

Take accountability for your own schedule. Make sure you only commit to tasks that you have time to do an ad that if you're stretched for time, you learn to prioritize and take responsibility for carving out time for the most important tasks.

3) Practice saying NO

Say no to temptation. No to other events going on. No to friends pressuring you to go out. No to yourself.

There is nobody else to blame when you procrastinate. Instead of waiting until after the inevitable to figure out where it all went wrong, take responsibility before it gets that far.

Tell yourself and others 'no' when anybody— including yourself—tries to distract you from what you're doing.

4) Solve your own problems

Let's use Lucy as an example once again. Let's come back to her the day after her night out.

Lucy has finally got around to filling in her internship application. The deadline is in two days and she knows the competition is tough.

She's a third of the way through when she runs into an obstacle. There is a field for her to fill in her Social Security number.

Lucy balks. She lost her Social Security care during her move into this apartment and never got it replaced. She doesn't know what it is off the top of her head.

She groans and closes her laptop.
She'll have to come back to it later.

Lucy gave up at the first hurdle and did what procrastinators always do—put it off until later.

Why do you think she is doing this? Will the obstacle be less difficult later? Will her Social Security card magically show up?

By not deciding to be the solution to her own problem—by not taking personal accountability— she has once again put off the task, and that deadline's getting closer.

Lucy is telling herself there's nothing she can do. In her mind, the Social Security number is gone and it's out of her hands.

To take personal responsibility, Lucy needs to take control of this situation.

She could:

- Go back through old applications and documents to see where her Social Security number has appeared before
- Contact her parents to see if they have a copy of the information.

Lucy has now suffered the consequences of her procrastination twice. She put off applying for a new Social Security card when she lost her last one, and now when she needs the information, it's not available. Secondly, she put off her application until a few days before the deadline and has encountered an unexpected roadblock.

Think about a task or project you're putting off. Are you telling yourself there is a hurdle you can't overcome?

Take personal accountability for putting this task off. Do your research, seek support, and find a way to overcome the problem to move forward with what you need to do.

Recognizing the value of small successes

Many of us get overwhelmed by the prospect of big commitments, such as switching jobs, implementing lifestyle changes, or developing a skill that takes time.

Let's remember Carl's situation.

Carl weighs in at 362lbs. He's got to lose about 200lbs to be a healthy weight.

What're the chances of him ever getting that done?

He's never going to reach his target weight, so he can't find the motivation to lose any weight at all.

For Carl, he fell into the trap of all-or-nothing, and this is a common pitfall for people trying to commit to a large lifestyle change or a pursuit that requires long-term effort and dedication.

There are ways to change this mindset.

1) Celebrate small victories

Carl has been putting off starting a diet because 200lbs seems like a mountain. He is not visualizing the benefits of losing some weight, even if he doesn't lose all 200lbs.

According to the Centers for Disease Control and Prevention, even losing 5% of your body weight can equal benefits to your health, including lowering risk factors for chronic obesity-related diseased (Centers for Disease Control and Prevention, n.d.)

For Carl, a 5% weight loss is only 18lbs—a fraction of his 200lbs goal.

Yet, Carl is not thinking about the benefits of the small victories. He is visualizing the process as a single goal.

2) **Break it down**

For lifestyle changes and big projects, it's important to break down goals into manageable chunks. Not only does this make it easier to manage your time and handle the project, but it also gives you a chance to celebrate victories along the way to achieving your bigger goal.

This can help shift perspective from one large and impossible goal to a number of smaller, realistic goals.

3) **Communicate your successes**

Bring others into celebrating your successes with you. If you lose 1lb or 2lb, celebrate this.

Being part of a community or social group on the same journey can help keep you motivated and heading in the right direction—this is one of the reasons why weight loss groups attract so many participants.

4) Keep track of your successes

Don't let your achievements—however small—get swept under the carpet and forgotten about.

Find a way to monitor and recognize these.

In Carl's situation, he could use a fitness app to track his calories and monitor his weight loss.

For other situations, other methods of tracking can be used.

Compassion for the future you

Tom is what most of us might imagine when we think of a procrastinator. Remember him?

> *Tom stretches and sits back with a*
> *smile on his face. He could work on*
> *his thesis…but he'll do it next week.*

Tom puts off working on his thesis because he makes it the responsibility of his future self.

He does not consider what pressures his future self might be facing or how things might change in the future.

He does not consider what it will be like to be under pressure, stressed, and worried in the future. He shows no compassion for his future self.

The Atlantic describes self-control as empathy with your future self. (Yong, 2016). In fact, science has shown that the same part of the brain that controls empathy, also controls self-control. This is why self-control and empathy are almost impossible to separate; the person you are showing empathy for is yourself. The future you.

Connection to your future self: why does it matter?

A 2011 study in the *Journal of Consumer Research* outlines a study in which college students were asked to assess whether their upcoming graduation would represent a major life change or only a trivial one. Those who saw their graduation as a significant event were able to exercise greater self-control in the present than those who didn't think that their graduation was a big deal. (Columbia Business School, 2011).

Being able to visualize and recognize the importance of future endeavors has been proven to increase your ability to exercise self-control in the present.

For procrastinators, this is an important skill to learn.

Develop a long-term mindset

One way of developing compassion for your future self is to develop a long-term mindset.

Part of the reason why procrastinators burden their future selves is because they don't see the harm in putting those responsibilities on their future shoulders.

However, every action in the present has an effect in the future.

Ask yourself: how will putting off this task now affect my wellbeing in the future? Will it create extra stress or pressure? Will it take away time you'll need for other things going on at that time?

Recognize your future self as a dependent

Your future self is entirely dependent on your actions for their wellbeing.

The more preparation, work, and effort you put in now take the burden off of yourself in the future.

Picture the following:

Thursday evening

8:00pm   *Martha makes some pasta for tomorrow's lunch. She packs it up in a plastic tub and places it in the fridge.*

08:30pm   *Martha chooses what she's going to wear the next day and hangs it on the back of the door.*

09:00pm   *Martha sets the coffee machine to come on at 06:30am the next day.*

Friday morning

06:30am   *Martha wakes up to the smell of freshly brewed coffee. She sits on her porch with a cup of hot coffee and enjoys the sunrise for fifteen minutes.*

06:45am   *Martha showers brush her teeth and dry her hair. She doesn't stress about what she should wear. Her clothes are already chosen. She gets dressed.*

07:15   *Martha grabs her lunch from the fridge and*

heads out the door with a bounce in her
step.

What we see here is how Martha's compassion for her future self has allowed her to wake up on a Friday morning ready, prepared and stress-free. And who has she got to thank for the easy morning? Her past self.

Imagine if her past self had not been so generous.

Friday morning

06.30am   *Martha wakes up and heads downstairs to put the kettle on. The coffee machine takes forever to work, so she has instant coffee instead. She's got to make lunch so it gets cold before she has a chance to drink it.*

06:45am   *Martha doesn't have time to cook fresh, healthy pasta in the morning, so she puts together a sandwich out of what she's got leftover in the fridge. It puts her in a bad mood. She looks forward to lunchtime all morning, and all she's got is stale bologna.*

07:00   *Martha steps out the shower and looks at her wardrobe in despair. She's got no idea what to wear. She looks at her watch and realizes she's got left in fifteen minutes. She grabs an outfit quickly out of the wardrobe. She scowls at her reflection in the mirror. She looks so frumpy.*

Martha's morning got off to a bad start because her past self left her to get everything done. She didn't get to enjoy the sunset, her coffee was cold, her lunch sucked, and she felt self-conscious all day in her un-ironed clothes.

Every decision you make in the present has a consequence for your future self.

Is procrastination now worth the struggle you're putting on the shoulders of your future self later?

Be as generous to yourself as you are others

Let's look at a new case study.

> *Amy's boyfriend has just moved in with her.*
>
> *She adores looking after him. Every evening she cooks him a delicious meal, she prepares his lunches for work with cute little notes inside, and she always makes sure the dishes are done before he gets home from work.*
>
> *She wants him to be relaxed and happy. She loves him and enjoys taking care of him.*

Amy would do anything for her boyfriend. She considers his wellbeing her responsibility and a priority. She's willing to put herself out to make his life easier.

Showing compassion to your future self should be a reflection of the same kind of generosity and love.

Amy will prepare dinner for her boyfriend, but she won't pay those bills now so that her future self can relax.

See your future self as an individual entity and love and be generous towards them. The future you will thank you for it!

Overcoming procrastination and maintaining momentum

Why do we relapse into bad habits?

You found the willpower to start that diet after procrastinating for months. For weeks, everything was going well, and then you gave in and binged one night. Since then, you've found it hard to get back into it and the weight is starting to pile back on.

Relapse is something that many procrastinators struggle with. For the procrastinator, it's hard enough to get started on a project, lifestyle change or big project without having to find the willpower to do it again because they've fallen off the wagon.

But what is it that makes us relapse into bad habits when we've managed to get on track?

Here are some of the most common culprits:

- **Reward mentality** — a person who struggles to get motivated and has a tendency to procrastinate may also have a tendency to motivate themselves with rewards. The problem with rewards is the likelihood of temptation.

  For example, a dieter who has counted calories for weeks without slipping up may feel they deserve a reward. They decide they're going to eat a donut. However, before they know it, they've eaten all four in the pack.

Rewarding yourself for small victories is not inherently a bad thing, but it is important to ensure that the rewards you choose complement the path you're on. If you are a dieter, for example, a food-based reward can be the trigger that causes you to break self-control. Another option could be buying a new item of clothing in your new, smaller size. This reward recognizes your achievement but doesn't tempt you into breaking the good habit you've worked hard to develop.

- **Too much self-confidence** — Everything has been going well for a long time. You haven't missed a deadline, you're on track; you have complete faith in your own self-discipline and willpower.

  The problem arises when your willpower actually falters at the moment.

  Willpower must be a constant exercise.

- **Forgetting intention** — Why did you start on this lifestyle change, project, or task in the first place?

  Sometimes procrastinators who've maintained a good habit for a long time can relapse because they've forgotten the big picture, the values at the core of their attempt, or the reason behind their main goal.

For example, a young woman dieter may have begun in order to look beautiful on her wedding day. A professional in the workplace may be working hard on a nighttime course in order to get a promotion, a raise, and ultimately to afford a better lifestyle.

When we get lost in the drudgery and boredom of good habit, we can forget that we're committing to this endeavor in order to reap the reward of our efforts. Taking the time to remind yourself why you're doing what you're doing can help you to stay on track.

- **A moment of weakness** — Many people who've been working for a long time towards an end goal find that they occasionally give into temptation. For some, the realization that they've had a lapse of self-control is enough to send them into a tailspin. That one muffin on a diet becomes a 4,000 calorie binge; that half an hour nap during the day becomes an afternoon in front of the TV.

  It is important to let a moment of weakness be just that—a moment. It is incredibly easy to backslide if we let our guilt and frustration convince us that all is lost.

No progress that has been made is ever lost because you momentarily give into temptation. Five pounds lost is still five pounds lost even if you have that cupcake. 5,000 words towards a dissertation are still 5,000 words, even if you end up giving in to peer pressure and going out to party on a night you'd planned to work.

Consider whether you've let a moment of weakness turn into a relapse. Take count of all you achieved before this point, remind yourself of your early intentions, and start again immediately.

Know your triggers

1) Think about what has caused you to relapse before.

We've already seen examples of relapse in our case studies in this book. Remember Judy? For her, the trigger was an invite to a night out.

If Judy found herself in a similar situation in the future, she could use this experience to prevent making the same mistake again. If an invite from her

roommate caused her to procrastinate in the past, then it can be reasoned that she might do the same in the future.

Therefore, she could predict the temptation, or 'trigger', and take steps to avoid being in the same situation again. For example, instead of completing her application in a shared apartment, she could take her work to a local library or coffee shop.

2) Avoid enablers

An enabler is any person who encourages a bad habit. For Judy, her enabler was her roommate who encouraged her to go out.

For Carl, it may be his mom who cooks amazing homecooked meals.

Anyone who encourages to break from a commitment you've made to self-improvement or personal progress enables you to procrastinate and prevents you from achieving your goals.

Enablers may be friends, partners, colleagues, or relatives. The trick is to avoid enablers at times when it is important you focus.

Try scheduling time with these people around your important tasks, and practice the habit of preloading your decisions.

Remember, preloading decisions is the practice of making decisions in a cool state before you are faced with temptation or distraction.

For example, Just could have already practiced her response to what she might say if her roommate tries to encourage her to go out, e.g. "I'm sorry, but if I don't do this now, I'm going to struggle later. I'm free on Tuesday night. Let's grab a drink then."

Recognize the signs of a relapse

1) Recognize urges

Take account of that niggling feeling of temptation that works its way into our mind when we've been experiencing success in our pursuit of good and healthy habits.

For the dieter, this may be a craving for a packet of crisps or chocolate bar. For the student, it may be the feeling of 'I could *really* do with a night out.'

When these urges strike, take time to recognize and address them immediately.

Remind yourself of the value of what you're doing and why the long-term benefits of sticking to plan outweigh the pleasure of immediate gratification.

2) Take account of your emotions

We've discussed hot and cold states earlier in this book. We know that in a cold state we are at our most focused and calm, while in a hot state we may be distracted by any number of internal emotions and external factors.

Learn to recognize when you are shifting from a cold state to a hot state. Are you beginning to feel angry, frustrated, disheartened or experiencing a nosedive in your self-esteem?

When you feel yourself entering a hot state, take practical steps to prevent this from escalating.

Drink some water, take a short walk, put on some calming music, take five minutes to have a phone call with a friend...Remaining in the cold state is key to being able to focus and make progress.

However, make sure you balance your self-care with self-discipline. Don't let that five-minute phone call turn into an hour-long gossip session. Don't let that relaxing music coax you into a nap.

Do what you can to preserve your cold state, but also recognize when you have actually crossed a line from maintaining calm to encouraging procrastination.

3) Making excuses

We've spoken about the usefulness and importance of personal accountability in the fight against procrastination.

One of the warning signs that you are facing a relapse into bad habits is when you start to make excuses for why you can't do what you set out to do.

For example:

- "I can't exercise today. It's pouring down with rain."

- "I couldn't read that book. The kids were banging around upstairs and I couldn't hear myself think."

- "I can't do a unit of the course tonight. I've got too much housework to do."

- "There was no point working on my essay last night. Everybody in the house was using the internet and the wifi was slow. I decided it made more sense to wait until everyone was out of the house."

Sound familiar? Chronic procrastinators are masterful excuse-makers and can always find a reason why they *couldn't* do what needed to be done.

Someone who is on track and maintaining good habits doesn't make excuses; they find solutions.

If you are someone who regularly makes excuses as a reason to procrastinate, start practicing having an internal dialogue with yourself when those excuses start to manifest.

For example:

- "I can't exercise today. It's pouring down with rain."

  - *"That's an excuse. I have YouTube. There are tons of free workout videos on there. I'll do for twenty minutes in my bedroom.*

- "I couldn't read that book. The kids were banging around upstairs and I couldn't hear myself think."

  - *That's an excuse. There's no reason I can't go up to my bedroom where it's quieter, put in a pair of earphones, or ask my husband to occupy the kids for an hour. This is important.*

- "I can't do a unit of the course tonight. I've got too much housework to do."

  - *That's an excuse. I've had all day to do housework and instead I watched TV. If the housework was that important, I would have done it earlier. I promised myself I was going to work on my course tonight, and that's what I'm going to do. The course is my priority.*

- "There was no point working on my essay last night. Everybody in the house was using the internet and the wifi was slow. I decided it made more sense to wait until everyone was out of the house."

- o *That's an excuse. Every time I start my essay I get distracted and find a reason to stop. I can work on the bits that don't need internet sources so at least I'm doing something or I could go out to the college library and use the internet there.*

Notice that in these imagined responses, we've deliberately included the phrase 'That's an excuse'.

This is a phrase you need to learn to tell yourself. We can always find reasons not to do that thing we've been avoiding, but as soon as we start calling ourselves out for this behavior, it becomes easy to recognize that many of our reasons are simply excuses.

Keeping track of your successes

Being able to monitor and recognize your successes is one of the positives of avoiding procrastination. Procrastinators are constantly faced with the consequences of delaying what needs to get done — low self-esteem, poor reputations, time pressures, stress, fatigue… It's a wonderful thing to be able to track and recognize all that you accomplish when you overcome your habit of procrastination.

Let your own successes be your motivation to stay on track. They are proof that procrastination has been holding you back for too long and allow you to recognize all you can achieve when being your most productive.

The Bullet Journal Method

Journaling is a popular method for setting goals and recording achievements.

A journal can read like a personal diary, or more like a calendar.

Bullet journaling, in particular, is becoming an increasingly popular method for young people to organize their lives and keep track of their goals and accomplishments.

The Bullet Journal was a crowdsourced initiative created by Ryder Carroll, a digital product designer who found that his learning disabilities often held him back from being able to be focused and productive.

The Bullet Journal, or BoJo for short, was created to help him and others like him to organize their lives and master 'the art of intentional living'. (Bullet Journal, n.d.)

The Bullet Journal is described as 'a mindfulness practice disguised as a productivity system. It's designed to help you organize your 'what' while you remain aware of your 'why'. (Bullet Journal, n.d.)

A Bullet Journal can be purchased online, or you can also make use of the companion app which includes a reflection tracker and guide.

You can also purchase Carroll's book on the bullet journal method—*The Bullet Journal Method.*

Apps

In this age of modern technology, what better way is there to keep track of your accomplishments that an app?

The benefit of a phone app is that it goes with you wherever you go, making it incredibly easy to carry your goals in your pocket and track your accomplishments on the go.

There are several apps that can be used for this purpose.

Here are a few that are gaining popularity:

- **The Way of Life App** — The Way of Life is a habit tracker app that logs your goals and allows you to record their completion. (Way of Life, n.d.)

- **Asana** — Asana is an organizational app that allows you to plan and structure work by setting priorities and deadlines for yourself and tracking your completion of these tasks. (Asana, n.d.)

- **Clear Todos** — Clear is a simple to-do list app that color-codes tasks according to urgency and offer on-screen reminders of the things you need to do. (Apple, n.d.)

- **Strides** — Strides is a habit tracker that allows you to track both your positive and negative habits. One of its most attractive features is its progress graphs and charts, which are great for those who like an easy visual representation of their progress. (Strides, n.d.)

- **HabitBull** — HabitBull is a multi-faceted app that allows you to communicate with a community of people pursuing goals, track your accomplishment data, and receive reminders for tasks to be done.

These are just a handful of available apps we uncovered with our research but there are hundreds available, and many are completely free. They may be labeled as 'to do apps', habit trackers, or productivity tools.

Try searching Google Play or the App Store to find an app that works best for you.

The Seinfeld Method

The Seinfeld Method is a simple but effective means of tracking your progress—and all you need is a wall calendar.

The idea is simple. You set your goal, and every day you accomplish what you set out to do, you check off that date on the calendar, to create a visual representation of your 'chain' of successes.

The idea is to not break the chain.

Brad Isaac, who claims to have been personally given this advice from Jerry himself, summarizes the effect of this method in the following way:

"Daily action builds habits. It gives you practice and will make you an expert in a short time. If you don't break the chain, you'll start to spot opportunities you otherwise wouldn't. Small improvements accumulate into large improvements rapidly because daily action provides "compounding interest.

[...] Think for a moment about what action would make the most profound impact on your life if you worked it every day." (Trapani, 2007)

This is a great method for those who enjoy a personal challenge. It's also one of the more light-hearted suggestions in this book.

If Jerry Seinfeld recommends it, it's got to be good!

Start each day from zero

LaunchDarkly CEO Edith Harbaugh uses this technique to allow her to visualize her success on a daily basis. (MacKay, 2018)

Huge goals can be so monumental that daily achievements can feel insignificant. For example, if we remember Carl, losing 1lb of his 200lb target can feel like nothing at all. However, if his daily goal was to stay beneath 1,800 calories, and he achieved this, he has a reason to celebrate.

In order to start each day from zero, you need to first decide how you are going to quantify your progress.

Like Carl, this may be a calorie count. For a writer, it may be a word count. For a marketer, it may be the number of social media posts, likes, or retweets they generate.

Whatever your big goal is, find a way to quantify what you do each day that contributes towards the success of this larger goal.

This helps keep you motivated and reassures you that you are chipping away at that bigger goal. It means you are not holding out for the satisfaction of that one big win, but celebrating all the small daily victories.

Step By Step 66 Day Plan: Daily Mantras and Challenges

The following pages are to be read at a pace of one a day to help the procrastinator recognize their habit, develop willpower, and focus on the task at hand.

Why 66 mantras?

A 2009 study of 96 volunteers found that, on average, it takes 66 days to break a habit. (al, 2010)

These mantras are a challenge. Can you break the habit of procrastination in 66 days?

You'll notice that each mantra comes with a daily challenge to complete. Pay attention to how the challenge is phrased—this is *today's* challenge. Every challenge that accompanies the following mantras should be completed on the same day it is read.

How to use this section

You can focus these challenges around as many or as few tasks, changes, or projects as you wish. You may be reading this book to give you the push you need to face one particularly large challenge, or you may be generally trying to break the habit of procrastination.

Whatever your motivation, use this resource as it works best for you. You can revisit it as many times as you need, reread it as often as you'd like. You may find certain challenges work really well in tackling certain forms of procrastination, or that some resonate more strongly with you while others do not seem so helpful.

Remember to use the mantras in conjunction with the challenges. These have been included to help you change the way you think about the challenges you face, the value of facing these challenges head-on, and the downfalls of choosing to delay.

Track your successes

You can use one of the methods for tracking successes from the previous chapter to monitor your progress. Remember, you are trying to break the habit of procrastination.

Maybe try the Seinfeld method. Each day you achieve the day's challenge, you can check off that date.

How long can you go without breaking the chain?

All quotes retrieved from: (Fabrega, https://daringtolivefully.com/procrastination-quotes) unless otherwise stated.

Day One

"Nothing is so fatiguing as the eternal hanging on of an uncompleted task."

~ William James

Many of us will often put off something important because we imagine how draining that task will be. However, in reality, the weight of an unfinished task is its own burden, often far more draining than the task itself.

Today's challenge: Make a list of tasks or changes you've been putting off. In what ways are the things you've listed creating extra stress or pressure in your life? How would things improve if these things weren't hanging over you?

Day Two

"You may delay, but time will not."

~ Benjamin Franklin

Deadlines are generally inflexible, and time is fleeting. The time will pass whether you are working towards your goal or not. Procrastinating only brings you closer to that deadline with nothing to show for the time that has passed.

Today's challenge: Set a goal to complete a quantifiable portion of a task, project or change you've been putting off, today. Choose how you will measure your progress before you begin. Are you aiming for a particular word count? An amount of time spent on a task? A target number of something? However, you choose to quantify your progress, ensure you have something to work towards whose result can be measured. Achieve this goal today.

Day Three

"To think too long about doing a thing often becomes its undoing."

~ Eva Young

Many procrastinators defend their procrastination as preparation, but preparation is only useful if it supports progress towards a goal. When there is preparation without progress, what actually remains is procrastination.

Today's challenge: Revisit the 'preparations' towards an old goal. Make a start towards that goal even if you do not feel prepared.

Day Four

"Procrastination is opportunity's assassin."

~ Victor Kiam

Procrastinators constantly let opportunities pass them by because they're always putting things off. Often, by the time the procrastinator gets around to acting on their desire, they find the opportunity has passed.

Today's challenge: Pursue an opportunity related to your goal. For example, if you're a dieter, you could join a dieting forum or weight loss group. If you're a student, you could attend a non-compulsory lecture. If you're a working professional, you could volunteer for extra duty at work. Whatever your goal,your challenge today is to seek out and commit to an opportunity that will help you succeed in that goal.

Day Five

"If you want to make an easy job seem mighty hard, just keep putting off doing it."

~ Olin Miller

Every procrastinator knows that the longer a task is put off, the harder it becomes to complete. Deadlines create time pressures, and our own guilt creates stress. We often find our personal circumstances worsening while we wait for motivation to fall from the sky and push us into action.

Today's challenge: Think of a task you've been putting off. List at least three ways in which the task will become more difficult the longer you put it off.

Day Six

"The best way to get something done is to begin."

~ Author Unknown

This mantra is an excellent go-to line that all procrastinators should have in their resource bank. Many procrastinators are perfectionists who spend a long time preparing for a task they never begin. Think of all the times you've bought new equipment for a hobby you never got into, or all the times you've dreaded starting a task that went quicker than you imagined. The only way to defeat procrastination is to move past it, push it aside, and get started.

Today's challenge: Start something you've been putting off, whether that be from your personal or professional life. Maybe there is a hobby you wanted to learn but never got around to developing the skill. Maybe you're ready for a life change, but it's never felt like quite the right time to begin. Today is the day.

Day Seven

"A year from now you may wish you had started today."

~ Karen Lamb

Groupon is a deals site and app that works alongside companies to offer deals on products, services, and experiences to people worldwide. It is currently valued at around $1 billion. How long did it take to reach this value?

Two years.

A little time can make a big difference. That small business idea you've been nurturing forever might be the start of something huge. That diet you haven't started could see you drop three dress sizes in a year. That promotion you haven't gone for? Next year you could be earning twice your current salary.

Procrastination only delays the time it takes to see the rewards of our efforts. The sooner you put in the effort, the sooner you can reap the benefits.

Today's challenge: What big change would make the greatest difference in your life a year from now? Identify the area of your life in which you struggle the most. Perhaps you're experiencing problems in your relationship. Perhaps money is a worry. Perhaps you hate being stuck in a dead-end job.

Identify what part of life is the least satisfying and create a plan—*today*—for how you will improve this situation within the next year.

Day Eight

> *"Procrastination is the thief of time."*

> ~ Edward Young

If productivity is the gift of time, then procrastination is surely the thief. When time is spent well, it can be used to create wonderful life experiences, work towards major goals, and improve our lives for the better. When wasted away through procrastination, time simply passes and nothing changes.

Today's challenge: Schedule an hour of your day to do something truly productive.

Day Nine

"Procrastination usually results in sorrowful regret. Today's duties put off until tomorrow give us a double burden to bear; the best way is to do them in their

111

proper time."

~ Ida Scott Taylor

This quote brings us back to the idea of compassion for your future self. Everything you put off until later, you're putting straight onto the shoulders of your future self.

Today's challenge: Do something to benefit your future self. Prepare lunch ready for tomorrow. Start a project a day early. Do that laundry now.

Day Ten

"Following-through is the only thing that separates dreamers from people that accomplish great things".

~ Gene Hayden

Gagan Biyani was working for the government in Washington D.C when he realized he wasn't doing what he wanted to do with his life. He had an interest in technology but no experience and no network. Over the next several months, he read the TechCrunch blog daily, and when a job opening was advertised a few months later, he applied and got the job. At the same time, he joined the Founder Institute, a startup incubator for aspiring entrepreneurs.

His initial startup idea failed, but through his networking at the Founder Institute, he met the man who would be his co-founder for Udemy, a site for online learning that is now worth approximately $710 million.

(Biyani, 2015)

Biyani was a tech amateur with no funding and no network to help him succeed. Through sheer determination and daily commitment, he created a name for himself in the tech industry, effectively networked, and co-founded a start-up that went on to be worth hundreds of millions.

Today's challenge: Make a list of what is holding you back from following through on a life change, a project or other task. Research and plan how you are going to tackle these obstacles. Like Biyani, is there a daily habit you can undertake to help move you towards your goal? Is there something you can teach yourself or a network you can build to help you achieve your goals?

Day Eleven

"Until you value yourself, you will not value your time. Until you value your time, you will not do anything with it."

~ M. Scott Peck

Low self-esteem is common among procrastinators. Many of us put off the things we should be doing because we don't have faith we will do them well.

Today's challenge: Make a list of your three greatest accomplishments and your three greatest strengths. Tell yourself that you, and your time, are valuable.

Day Twelve

"If you put off everything till you're sure of it, you'll never get anything done."

~ Norman Vincent Peale

Self-doubt can be crippling and often comes hand-in-hand with the psychology of procrastination. Someone may put off starting a university course because they're worried whether or not they'll find a career they enjoy at the end of it. A man might put off a proposal because he's worried about commitment.

Sometimes, the life choices we face are huge. Phenomenally huge. This can leave us frozen, putting off all of the big choices forever because it's too scary to commit to one path.

Being too reckless can result in making decisions that are ultimately bad for us, but being too cautious can result in our lives coming to a standstill.

It is important to be able to differentiate between whether we are holding off because a choice is the wrong one, or because we are simply too scared to take the leap into something that could lead to wonderful things.

Today's challenge: Think of one of the biggest life decisions you've ever made. Do you recall how you felt at the time? Was there uncertainty? Was there a doubt? Are there any lessons from that previous experience that you could apply to a decision you are currently facing?

Day Thirteen

> *"Someday is not a day of the week."*

~ Janet Daily, (Daily, n.d.)

Procrastinators often use vague descriptions of time to avoid committing to a task. A procrastinator will often schedule tasks for 'later', 'tomorrow', 'in a bit', or 'soon'. This vagueness leaves a lot of room for plans to change and procrastination to seep in.

Today's challenge: Schedule a task you are going to complete today. Choose the time and place you are going to do this task and stick to it.

Day Fourteen

"Begin to weave and God will give you the thread."

~ German Proverb

The English equivalent of this proverb is 'God helps those who helps himself'. In short, you have to be the creator of your own success. It is the effort you put into a task that creates results.

Today's challenge: Identify three ways you can help yourself today. It may be a simple preparation task, such as doing some research for a paper. Maybe you're facing financial difficulties; perhaps some research into a savings account will be helpful. Think of where you're struggling and find a way to help yourself.

Day Fifteen

"Often greater risk is involved in postponement than in making a wrong decision."

~ Harry A. Hopf

Procrastination always has consequences. Some of them were outlined at the beginning of this book—increased stress and pressure, insomnia, poor self-esteem, a decline in work quality, wasted time, missed opportunities and failing to reach your own full potential, to name a few.

Today's challenge: Identify one of the consequences you may face if you put off an important task today.

Day Sixteen

"The habit of always putting off an experience until you can afford it, or until the time is right, or until you know how to do it is one of the greatest burglars of joy. Be deliberate, but once you've made up your mind -jump in."

~ Charles R. Swindoll

Procrastinators always find a reason to wait. But what if there is no good reason? What if you've saved the money, you have the time, or all the conditions are just right? Why then are you holding off?

Today's challenge: Identify a task you've been putting off. List the reasons you've been putting off this task. Are these genuine reasons to postpone, or are you unnecessarily putting off taking the leap?

Day Seventeen

"Getting an idea should be like sitting on a pin; it should make you jump up and do something."

~ E. L. Simpson

Procrastinators often struggle to get motivated to tackle tasks because they don't have the enthusiasm to pursue what is in front of them.

Today's challenge: Choose a task you've been putting off. How can you reframe your perception of this task to harness motivation? If the task itself seems dull, visualize the reward. What can you do to generate some excitement about this task?

Day Eighteen

"There is nothing so fatal to character as half-finished tasks."

~ David Lloyd George

Whenever a task is left unfinished, the potential accomplishment that could have been achieved is lost. Over time, unfinished tasks can lead to a sense of failure and low self-esteem, when in reality, the ability to complete these tasks has always been there.

Today's challenge: Finish a half-finished task, however big or small it may be.

Day Nineteen

"Don't wait. The time will never be just right."

~ Napoleon Hill

Perfectionist procrastinators want every condition to be perfect before they take a leap, such as submitting that application, setting off on that new venture, or making a big change. However, sometimes there is no right time. We have to adapt to the conditions as they are.

Today's challenge: Find one way to adapt to your current situation in order to make progress towards a goal.

Day Twenty

"Doing just a little bit during the time we have available puts you that much further ahead than if you took no action at all."

~Byron Pulsifer

In Chapter Eleven, we explored the importance of celebrating small successes. This quote reiterates the idea that every small step counts towards that big goal.

There is no victory too small to be recognized and celebrated.

Today's challenge: Identify one achievement from your week so far and celebrate it.

Day Twenty-One

> *"Stop talking. Start walking."*

> ~ L.M. Heroux

What's the use in huge dreams if we never take active steps to pursue them? It's time to put words into actions and ideas into practice.

Today's challenge: Take one step today to put an idea, goal, or dream into practice.

Day Twenty-Two

> *"We all sorely complain of the shortness of time, and yet have much more than we know what to do with. Our lives are either spent in doing nothing at all, or in doing nothing to the purpose, or in doing nothing that we ought to do. We are always complaining that our days are few, and acting as though there would be no end of them."*

> ~ Lucius Annaeus Seneca

Time wasted does not equal a lack of time. We all have time to achieve great things. Think of those people who seem to be able to do it all—the local supermom who keeps fit, raises three kids, and runs her own business; or the college student who works two part-time jobs and is class president. The difference between these great achievers and those who don't reach their goals is that they learn to use their time productively.

Today's challenge: Keep a diary of your activity today, divided into thirty-minute segments. Be completely honest. At the end of the day, review this diary. How much time was 'wasted' time, or time not used productively?

Day Twenty-Three

"When there is a hill to climb, don't think that waiting will make it smaller."

~Author Unknown

The dread of the task ahead often leads procrastinators to delay. However, delaying tasks does not make it easier to tackle. The hill will always be just as high.

Today's challenge: Think of a hill you need to climb. Divide the journey into a series of smaller steps and set deadlines for each step.

Day Twenty-Four

"To do anything in this world worth doing, we must not stand back shivering and thinking of the cold and danger, but jump in and scramble through as well as we can."

~ Syndey Smith

This is good advice for the anxious procrastinator. We know the anxious procrastinator does all they can to avoid entering the state of anxiety, but sometimes this type of procrastinator has to face their fears. The same goes for the perfectionist procrastinator who dreads not being good enough

Today's challenge: Do one thing today to confront anxiety related to your goal.

Day Twenty-Five

"Delay not to seize the hour!"

~ Aeschylus

Carpe Diem. Seize the day. Seize the hour.

Each day holds so much potential, but the procrastinator lets this potential go to waste.

Today's challenge: Start the day by writing down two ways the day can go. In the first list, you spend the day doing the bare minimum. In the second list, you max out your productivity. What do your lists reveal about how much potential you are letting slip by each day?

Day Twenty-Six

"So what do we do? Anything. Something. So long as we just don't sit there. If we screw it up, start over. Try something else. If we wait until we've satisfied all the uncertainties, it may be too late."

~ Lee Iacocca

This quote relates very well to the all-or-nothing procrastinator; the procrastinator who thinks the goal is too insurmountable, the time too long and the effort too great. Remember, every small effort counts. Every tiny step in the right direction chips away at the huge goal, until piece by piece, we resculpt our lives into our vision of perfection.

Today's challenge: Do one thing today to chip away at a larger goal.

Day Twenty-Seven

"This one makes a net, this one stands and wishes. Would you like to make a bet which one gets the fishes."

~ Chinese Rhyme

The one who acts goes further than the one who simply dreams. Procrastinators can spend a lot of time thinking, dreaming and wishing about how things could be, but always put off taking steps to make it happen.

Today's challenge: What would be the 'making a net' of your current situation? What is one practical thing you could do to facilitate your own success?

Day Twenty-Eight

"Begin doing what you want to do now."

~ Marie Beynon Ray

It's a simple message that procrastinators make hard. If you want something, why are you waiting?

Procrastinators do not only put off professional and academic goals but often put off investing in pursuits to fulfill them in their personal life because they let everything else take priority.

Today's challenge: Focus on a task that is not a need, but a want. What have you been putting off doing that is purely for your own interest, pleasure, or wellbeing? Give yourself some time today to focus on that task.

Day Twenty-Nine

"A primary reason people don't do new things is that they want to do them perfectly – the first time. It's completely irrational, impractical, not workable – and yet, it's how most people run their lives. It's called Perfection Syndrome."

~ John-Roger and Peter McWilliams

This is a strong mantra for the perfectionist procrastinator who is often hard on themselves and naïve in expecting perfect results the first time.

Today's challenge: Recall a time you have given up on something because you weren't able to master is quickly enough. In hindsight, were you irrational to expect immediate success? Where would you be now if you had continued to develop that skill, or follow that pursuit? Do you regret giving up? How can you apply this lesson to a situation you are currently facing in your life?

Day Thirty

> *"If and When were planted, and Nothing grew."*

> ~ Proverb

Procrastination yields no results. The only action creates something worthwhile.

Today's challenge: What could you 'plant' to make something 'grow'? What habit could you start to form today that could produce results in a week, a month, six months, and a year?

_____

Day Thirty-One

> *"Procrastination is the grave in which opportunity is buried."*

> ~ Author Unknown

Opportunities don't always wait forever. There are many situations in which opportunity is delimited by time or some other criteria. For example, many promising and rewarding graduate schemes don't accept applicants who are over 25 years of age. You cannot travel to foreign countries with an expired passport.

There are many situations where opportunities for experiences and personal progress are lost because someone took too long to act.

Today's challenge: What is something you really want in life? What opportunities are open to you to pursue this? Create a list of relevant deadlines associated with this dream. i.e. Closing date of job post, closing date of the grant application, upper age limits on schemes, etc.

Day Thirty-Two

"We shall never have more time. We have and have always had, all the time there is. No object is served in waiting until next week or even until tomorrow. Keep going day in and day out. Concentrate on something useful. Having decided to achieve a task, achieve it at all costs."

~ Arnold Bennett

Bennet says it all in this quote. When you set your mind to something that is in your own interest, you must follow it through to the end. Procrastination only allows time to pass without achieving positive change.

Today's challenge: Don't let today pass without achieving something. Choose whether to achieve a small step towards a larger goal, or to achieve a smaller victory today.

Day Thirty-Three

"You don't have to see the whole staircase, just take the first step."

~ Martin Luther King, Jr.

Big tasks are daunting. Long roads seem endless. However, each step is its own victory. It is only necessary to focus on one step at a time.

Today's challenge: What is a long-term challenge you've been facing? Identify the next single step you can take towards achieving that goal.

_____

Day Thirty-Four

"Things may come to those who wait, but only the things left by those who hustle."

~ Abraham Lincoln

Some people seem to have it all. Procrastinators often look on at these people jealously, thinking they are especially lucky, favored, or talented. The truth is, it is those who put themselves out there, take action, and go for it who get rewarded. If you wait for an opportunity to fall into your lap, you may be waiting a very long time.

Today's challenge: Fast-forward on a scheduled task. Do something now you'd planned to do later.

Day Thirty-Five

> *"How soon not now, becomes never."*
>
> ~ Martin Luther

Procrastinators often cross the line from 'later' to 'never', such as the would-be dieter who is still putting on weight although they've fantasized about dieting forever, or the aspiring writer who can never get past Chapter One.

Too many dreams gather dust on a shelf through procrastination.

Today's challenge: Revive a dream from the past. Revisit an old project that was never completed, a trip that was never taken, or contact a friend you've fallen out of touch with.

Day Thirty-Six

> *"The two rules of procrastination: 1) Do it today. 2) Tomorrow will be today tomorrow."*
>
> ~ Author Unkown, (Seale, n.d.)

This quote relates well to the hot-cold empathy gap explored in this book. We always assume we will have the willpower to do all those things we put on our shoulders for tomorrow, but too often we are faced with the fact that tomorrow, the willpower isn't there.

Today's challenge: Think back on the last time you procrastinated. How much did a lack of willpower play into the delay? Had you planned to do something later, then failed to do so because you weren't in the mood? How can you apply these lessons to a situation you're facing today?

Day Thirty-Seven

"All things come to those who wait, but when they come they're out of date."

~ Anonymous

Jenny saw a job advert online for her dream job. The salary was great. The location was perfect. The perks were awesome.

She deliberated for days over her resume, and then took a couple more days to decide whether or not to send it in.

At last, clicked 'send'. The next day, she gets a call from another company she'd applied for a week earlier. She accepts the offer and makes plans to move to the other side of the city to start work.

The day after she breaks the lease on her apartment, she hears back from the dream job to offer her an interview.

Today's challenge: Think of a task you've been putting off. What difference would it make if you saw the results of following through on that task in one month, six months, a year, or five years' time? What would you miss out on? What could you gain if you followed through today?

Day Thirty-Eight

"Work expands so as to fill the time available for its completion."

~ C. Northcote Parkinson

Procrastinators are experts at making short tasks last a long term. We are adept at finding distractions to delay the process and on focusing on the minutiae of a task to prevent us from really getting stuck in. Procrastinators can make a single task take a whole day.

Today's challenge: Think of a household chore you do regularly. What is the quickest you've ever done this chore? How long did it take when it took the longest? Ask yourself whether you're dragging tasks out at work or at home. What other things could you fit into the same time if you were more productive? What benefits would you reap from this?

Day Thirty-Nine

Do you know what happens when you give a procrastinator a good idea? Nothing!

~ Donald Gardner

Procrastinators are often bright, intelligent and creative people. Yet, procrastinators rarely reach the heights of their potential. Why? Because we are masters of inaction; the kings of delay.

Today's challenge: What is a good idea you've had in the past that you've never acted on? Review it now. Do you still think it's a good idea? How could you turn the idea into a reality?

Day Forty

"The search for the perfect venture can turn into procrastination. Your idea may or may not have merit. The key is to get started."

~ Unknown

Perfectionism and procrastination are often partners in crime. A great idea can be delayed again and again because its creators can only see its flaws and not its merit. The thing is, flaws can be worked out—but only by getting started.

Today's challenge: Write down an idea, project, or change you've been delaying. Beneath it, create a list of its flaws and the problems you foresee. Now they're on the page, start anyway. You know your idea isn't perfect, but getting started gives you opportunity to obtain the bigger picture and evaluate whether there is truly merit in the venture.

Day Forty-One

"It was my fear of failure that first kept me from attempting the master work. Now, I'm beginning what I could have started ten years ago. But I'm happy at least that I didn't wait twenty years."

~ Paulo Coelho

Paulo Coelho is the international best-selling author of *The Alchemist*. Before *The Alchemist* became successful, Coelho wrote three books that were flops. Even *The Alchemist* was withdrawn after 900 copies on its first run due to lack of public interest. It was only after the publication of his novel *Brida* that *The Alchemist* found some traction and gathered a huge fan following that escalated Coelho into the international spotlight. (Wikipedia, n.d.)

If Coelho had let his fear of failure stop him from starting his next novel, he would never have found the fame and recognition he eventually received.

Today's challenge: Is there a task you are putting off due to a fear of failure? Consider Coelho's success story and make another attempt.

Day Forty-Two

"The really happy people are those who have broken the chains of procrastination, those who find satisfaction in doing the job at hand. They're full of eagerness, zest, productivity. You can be, too."

~ Norman Vincent Peale

This book encourages you to monitor your progress and track your success because it is a rewarding practice. You will, in fact, find that I recognized your success you will be full of eagerness, zest, and productivity.

Today's challenge: Create a means of tracking your progress (in addition to the Seinfeld method).

Day Forty-Three

"You cannot plough a field by turning it over in your mind."

~ Author Unknown

Do not get stuck in the preparation stage of a new venture or existing project. It is a beartrap for the procrastinator.

Today's challenge: Make the move from the preparation stage to the actualization stage of a current project or venture.

135

Day Forty-Four

"I don't wait for moods. You accomplish nothing if you do that. Your mind must know it has got to get down to work."

~ Pearl S. Buck

This quote relates to partial naivete, the hot-cold empathy gap, and a lack of discipline. All three issues afflict the modern procrastinator.

For a procrastinator to break the habit of delay and make progress in his or her goals, they must avoid temptation, break away from distraction, and get down to work.

Today's challenge: Revisit Chapter Thirteen of this book. Identify and write down your own procrastination triggers. What can you do to better manage these when trying to get down to work?

Day Forty-Five

"Much of the stress that people feel doesn't come from having too much to do. It comes from not finishing what they started."

~ David Allen

The burden of unfinished tasks weighs heavily on procrastinators. As deadlines approach and incomplete tasks mount up, they can start to feel overwhelmed. If they completed tasks as they arose, they'd avoid much of the pressure they bring upon themselves.

Today's challenge: Make a list of the unfinished tasks on your to-do list. Try to organize these chronologically by when they first came to your attention. How many of those tasks could you have completed earlier to leave you with a smaller to-do list today?

Day Forty-Six

"If you believe you can accomplish everything by "cramming" at the eleventh hour, by all means, don't lift a finger now. But you may think twice about beginning to build your ark once it has already started raining."

~ Max Brooks

Many procrastinators live in 'crunch time'. They leave things to the last minute and then panic about how dire their situation has become.

Today's challenge: What would be the 'crunch time' of a current situation you are facing? How close are you to that crunch time? How can you avoid tackling the task at the eleventh hour?

Day Forty-Seven

"Somebody should tell us, right at the start of our lives, that we are dying. Then we might live life to the limit, every minute of every day. Do it! I say. Whatever you want to do, do it now! There are only so many tomorrows."

~ Michael Landon

Most of us think we are invincible; that the passing of time won't affect us. We don't think about how our circumstances might change in the near future. We never consider that life may not go to plan.

For the procrastinator, a plan gone awry is the worst possible thing that could happen, because it means all the things they were going to do are lost, and nothing they could have accomplished ever saw the light of day.

Today's challenge: Write down your bucket list. What do you want to do before you die? What do you want to experience while you have the time? What have you always wished you could do? Read and reread the list. Sit a while with the emotions you feel looking at them.

How would you feel in a year's time if you had checked off nothing of that list? What about in five years' time? Ten? Twenty?

Ask yourself whether you can afford to procrastinate and whether you could live with the regret of letting that bucket list become another pipe dream.

Day Forty-Eight

"He who every morning plans the transactions of that day and follows that plan carries a thread that will guide him through the labyrinth of the most busy life."

~ Victor Hugo

The organization is the procrastinator's best friend— when they have the discipline to stick to their plans.

Today's challenge: Write down a one-day plan to keep you on track towards a current goal. Make a list of people, things, or events that could deter you from following that plan.

Create a preloaded decision for each of these possibilities and stick to those throughout the day.

Day Forty-Nine

"Even if you're on the right track – you'll get run over if you just sit there."

~ Arthur Godfrey, (Develop Good Habits, 2019)

Procrastinators suffer the consequences of their own inaction. A great idea amounts to nothing if you don't follow it through.

Today's challenge: Identify a task where you started off strong but lost momentum. Which tips from this book can you implement to get back on track?

Day Fifty

"The certainty that life cannot be long, and the probability that it will be much shorter than nature allows, ought to awaken every man to the active prosecution of whatever he is desirous to perform. It is true, that no diligence can ascertain success; death may intercept the swiftest career; but he who is cut off in the execution of an honest undertaking has at least the honor of falling in his rank, and has fought the battle, though he missed the victory."

~ Samuel Johnson

Today's challenge: On Day Forty-Seven of this sixty-six-day plan, you wrote down your bucket list. Today, do one thing that will bring one of those dreams closer to reality.

Day Fifty-One

"Procrastination is the fear of success. People procrastinate because they are afraid of the success that they know will result if they move ahead now. Because success is heavy, carries responsibility with it, it is much easier to procrastinate and live on the "someday I'll" philosophy".

~ Denis Waitley

This book has looked at many examples of those who are afraid of failure. But what about those procrastinators who are afraid of success.

Let's look at an example:

Tammy has had her application for the volunteer 'Accommodation for Africa' scheme ready for weeks. When she first started the application, she was excited by the idea of three months in a foreign country, doing something good, meeting like-minded people, seeing the world, and getting something great to put on her resume. However, now the form is ready to submit, she's getting cold feet.

Has she really got what it takes to spend three months in Africa? What if she gets sick while she's out there? What if she misses home? What if she sucks at

*building houses and everybody resents
her? What if the social justice warriors
on social media accused her of having a
white savior complex?*

She's no longer sure she wants to apply.

Tammy has wanted to travel for years. Ever since she was sixteen she's been thinking about the day she graduates high school and can finally volunteer. She's followed the charity for years.

But now she's putting off sending off her application because she's afraid she'll get accepted and the responsibility and change will be too much to handle.

Today's challenge: Think of a time when you were scared of being successful. Did you follow through in the end? What were the results? Did you end up being happy? Did you end up learning something new? What was the butterfly effect of that choice? Did you ultimately end up being better or worse off for taking a leap of faith?

Day Fifty-Two

"If you have goals and procrastination you have nothing. If you have goals and you take action, you will have anything you want."

~ Thomas J. Vilord, (Develop Good Habits, 2019)

Visualizing success is not realizing success. You have to go through with your great visions to see the results of everything you've dreamed of.

Today's challenge: Take another action towards a goal today. Make sure to keep track of your successful completion of this step.

Day Fifty-Three

"Begin while others are procrastinating. Work while others are wishing."

~William Arthur Ward

To have what others don't, you have to do what others do not. Those who work the hardest yield the best results. Those who innovate and put themselves out there will never fail to reap the rewards.

Today's challenge: Step up for something that others aren't doing. Volunteer for a role at work. Offer to help a relative. Audition for a play. Do something to put yourself ahead.

Day Fifty-Four

"Don't procrastinate. Putting off an unpleasant task until tomorrow simply gives you more time for your

143

imagination to make a mountain out a possible molehill.
More time for anxiety to sap your self-confidence. Do it
now, brother, do it now."

~ Author Unknown

Dread seems to have a cumulative effect. The more you agonize about something, the worse it seems. Pulling off the bandaid is the best way to get past the fear.

Today's challenge: Pull off the bandaid on a situation you've been avoiding. Remember to employ the tactics outlined in Chapter Eight if you are suffering from an anxious state.

Day Fifty-Five

"Procrastination is a way for us to be satisfied with
second-rate results; we can always tell ourselves we'd
have done a better job if only we'd had more time. If
you're good at rationalizing, you can keep yourself
feeling rather satisfied this way, but it's a cheap happy.
You're whittling your expectations of yourself down
lower and lower."

~ Richard O'Connor

Procrastinators are professional coasters. They become experts on how to get by doing the bare minimum at the last minute. The problem with this is that we are only cheating ourselves. Each of us as beings of great potential. Procrastination steals that potential and makes us less than we are; less than we could be.

Today's challenge: Push yourself to a new limit today. Exercise until you feel the burn. Work on that project until your eyes begin to droop. Practice that instrument until your fingers are sore.

It is not healthy to push ourselves to extremes every day, but the fact is, we are all capable of coping with the discomfort of extra effort. A little extra effort every day translates to big results over time.

———————————————————————————

Day Fifty-Six

"Yesterday is a canceled check. Tomorrow is a promissory note. Today is the only cash you have, so spend it wisely."

~Kim Lyons

Procrastinators cannot get back the time they wasted yesterday and they can't predict how the day will unfold tomorrow. The only certain time they have is the time they have today. It is their responsibility to use it wisely and productively.

Today's challenge: Do something today that makes wise use of your time.

Day Fifty-Seven

"If we accept and internalize the fact of our own mortality, then, by definition, we have to deal with the essential questions of how we live and spend our allotted time. We have to stop procrastinating, pretending that we have forever to do what we want to do and be what we long to be."

~ Surya Das

Herman Melville, the author of Moby Dick, is said to have had his wife chain him to his desk daily while he was trying to finish his novel. (Procrastination and Science, n.d.)

Some of the greatest people throughout history have shown extraordinary amounts of self-control and discipline in order to achieve their goals; and their reward is recognition, fame, and being remembered throughout human history.

Today's challenge: What are you doing currently that is helping you become who you want to be or do what you want to do?

Day Fifty-Eight

> *"By one delay after another, they spin out their whole lives, till there's no more future left for them."*

> ~ Robert L'Estrange

Life is not made up of endless time. Although it's never too late to make a change, it's also ever too early to start.

Today's challenge: Do something today that counts towards a larger personal goal.

Day Fifty-Nine

> *"Delaying gratification is a process of scheduling the pain and pleasure of life in such a way as to enhance the pleasure by meeting and experiencing the pain first and getting it over with. It is the only decent way to live."*

> ~ M. Scott Peck

Immediate gratification is the habit of chronic procrastinators, while those who are able to delay gratification experience greater success in life.

Today's challenge: Working on the results of the Stanford Marshmallow Experiment, re-visualize a future result of a current project in a way that makes you recognize how it's worth the wait.

Day Sixty

"I have spent my days stringing and unstringing my instrument, while the song I came to sing remains unsung."

~ Rabindranath Tagore

Procrastinators are infamous for doing everything they can except what needs to be done. Over-preparation and completing endless small, less important tasks are hallmark habits of chronic procrastinators.

Today's challenge: What are your hallmark behaviors as a procrastinator? How do you usually find yourself getting distracted from your main task? Which smaller tasks do you end up prioritizing?

Write a list of these and keep them by you throughout the day. Every time you find yourself about to fall into one of the habitual behaviors, resist the urge and refocus on the task at hand.

Day Sixty-One

"Only put off until tomorrow what you are willing to die having left undone."

~ Pablo Picasso

Few of us are able to recognize what is truly important. We all make the mistake of assuming we have endless time; limitless tomorrows into which we can throw today's responsibilities. Every time we procrastinate, we risk turning a later into a never.

Today's challenge: Think about a time when procrastination led to you missing out on success in some way. What happened? What would have happened if you hadn't procrastinated?

Day Sixty-Two

"We are so scared of being judged that we look for every excuse to procrastinate."

~ Erica Jong

Fear of judgment can feed into a procrastinator's low self-esteem and encourage them to put off important work or changes.

Today's challenge: Think of a big task or change you've been avoiding. Make a list of all the ways you're afraid of being judged—by others, and by yourself.

Imagine a friend had come to you with their goal and a list of these worries. What would you tell them?

Support yourself the way you would support others and attempt to put that fear of judgment into perspective.

Day Sixty-Three

> *"He who hesitates is a damned fool."*

> ~ Mae West

Friends and relatives of procrastinators can be endlessly frustrated by seeing their loved one talk themselves out of opportunities and delay their own progress.

Today's challenge: Have a calm conversation with a friend or relative about a time when you have procrastinated. Ask them for what advice they would give for the future.

Day Sixty-Four

> *"Life, as it is called, is for most of us one long postponement."*

> ~ Henry Miller

The world is full of avid travelers who haven't discovered their passion because they've never got on a plane and talented artists who are undiscovered because they've never got around to finishing their work. If we could see our goals through to the end, so much more could be accomplished personally and globally.

Today's challenge: Think of an activity you have always wanted to try. Why have you been postponing this?

_____

Day Sixty-Five

> *"Time wasted is existence; used is life."*

> ~ Edward Young

If we fail to accomplish all that is within the reach of our potential, then we have failed to live our fullest and most rewarding lives.

Today's challenge: During the day, be aware of when you find yourself caught up in pursuing a mindless task, such as watching uninteresting TV, browsing your cell, or daydreaming. Make a conscious decision to use this time more productively, whether that is in a professional, academic, or creative pursuit.

_____

Day Sixty-Six

*"My biggest regret could be summed up in one word,
and that's procrastination."*

~ Ron Cooper

You have made it to the final day of the 66-day procrastination progress. Or maybe you did none of the tasks and skipped to the end...I hope not. This book has been designed to help the chronic procrastinator to become self-aware and proactive in order to achieve their goals.

If you've questioned whether or not to fully engage with this book, then take the above quote to heart. *My biggest regret could be summed up in one word, and that's procrastination.*

Today's challenge: Make an action plan for how you are going to continue combatting your procrastination over the next thirty days, employing all you have learned from this book.

Remember to keep track of your progress and successes, engage in proper self-care, and practice self-discipline where necessary.

You're on track for some great and positive changes. When you overcome procrastination, your potential is limitless.

Conclusion

Procrastination is a problem that presents itself in many different ways and has many different root causes— from the anxious procrastinator to the naïve one, from the perfectionist procrastinator to the rebel.

Understanding the deeper causes of our tendency to procrastinate is the key to releasing ourselves from its powerful grip.

This book was intended to help those who suffer from the consequences of procrastination in their daily lives, to guide you on your quest to making progress in your goals and changing your life for the better.

Take the time to read and reread this book as many times as you need to. Make the most of the mantras and challenges presented, and be prepared for some deep introspection.

But most of all, remember that it *is* possible to break free from the habit of procrastination to build a more productive and successful life.

PS: Thanks for reading: if you enjoyed this book, please consider leaving a short review on Amazon.